What Your Body Says (and how to master the message)

Inspire, Influence, Build Trust, and Create Lasting Business Relationships

Sharon Sayler

Illustrations by Amy Ruppel

WILEY

John Wiley & Sons, Inc.

Published by John Wiley & Sons, Inc., Hoboken, New Jersey.
Published simultaneously in Canada.

For general information on our other products and services or for technical support, please
contact our Customer Care Department within the United States at (800) 762-2974, outside
the United States at (317) 572-3993 or fax (317) 572-4002.

Wiley also publishes its books in a variety of electronic formats. Some content that appears in
print may not be available in electronic books. For more information about Wiley products,
visit our web site at www.wiley.com.

Library of Congress Cataloging-in-Publication Data:

Sayler, Sharon, 1956–
    What your body says (and how to master the message): inspire, influence,
build trust, and create lasting business relationships / Sharon Sayler;
illustrations by Amy Ruppel.
        p. cm.
    Includes bibliographical references.
    ISBN 978-0-470-59916-7 (cloth)
    ISBN 978-0-470-76985-0 (ebk)
    ISBN 978-0-470-76986-7 (ebk)
    ISBN 978-0-470-76987-4 (ebk)
    1. Body language.   2. Success in business.   I. Title.
    BF637.N66S29 2010
    153.6′9—dc22

                                                            2010012323

Printed in the United States of America.

10 9 8 7 6 5 4 3 2 1

With love to my sons, Adam and Jordan

This book is also dedicated to the many wonder-filled friendships I have enjoyed. I look forward to the adventure of many more that lie ahead.

Contents

Foreword

For more than a decade, Sharon and I have been colleagues. Our mutual interest in communication has led us to specialize in the nonverbals of interactions between individuals and within groups. We have pioneered methods to stabilize nonverbal patterns of communication and have collaborated in identifying the subtle patterns used by effective communicators across the globe.

Sharon is a liaison between our applied research and the public. By packaging practical ideas in an easy-to-apply format, readers will discover many *walk-away* new strategies from every chapter. Her conversational style provides access to many concepts that were buried in jargon-oriented books. Instead of case studies, she conveys insights through stories. Her focus is clear and her messages delivered with ease.

Yet Sharon is more than a liaison. Her book is full of original concepts, methods, charts, and inspiration. Sharon has expanded and enriched the field of nonverbal communication with new, practical patterns. Those who will benefit most from *What Your Body Says (and how to master the message)* are managers, mentors, trainers, teachers—literally everyone. Communication is challenging, even mysterious. Unpleasant surprises happen when well-intended messages are taken the wrong way. Words and nonverbals can send conflicting signals. Because the nonverbals of communication can either destroy or enhance careers and personal relationships, this book is important. It could change your life.

—Michael Grinder, author of 10 books, including
Managing Groups: The Fast Track and
Charisma: The Art of Relationships

Foreword

Wouldn't it be just brilliant if all our communication worked every time? Truth is, you're not going to be able to bat 1,000 percent. However, you can come pretty darn close. This book will help others receive your messages in the way you intended. Sharon Sayler's advice offered in the following pages of this book has helped me improve my communication skills and, most importantly, achieve my big goals.

If you want to do big things in the world, you have to be able to rally others to your cause or mission. If you want to lead a team, you've got to inspire others to share your vision. If you want to influence and guide your children so that their dreams are realized and their future is filled with success and happiness, you've got to inspire them. If you want a loving and supportive relationship, you've got to be courageous enough to express yourself authentically. This is all done through clear, compelling, and convincing communication.

I'm sure you've heard the old saying, "Long after people forget what you've done or said, they'll remember how you made them feel." I believe it's true.

What does your body say about you and how you make other people feel? At this moment, you may not know. However, after reading this book, you will. I relate to this book's methodology and its spirit. It is technically simple and straightforward, full of helpful, easy-to-follow advice and exercises. In addition, it's full of love, grace, and dignity. Sharon has accomplished something often missing from "how-to" books. She offers her expertise in ways that are always inspiring and empowering. She lives and breathes this stuff—she walks her talk and she talks her walk. Get it? Good. Now, you go get it so that you can share your true message with the world.

Get up, go on, and go out thinking bigger about who you are and what you offer the world. Of course, if you want to fulfill your big dreams, other people have to want to help you. In addition, if you become a masterful communicator, you'll have more offers of help than you know what to do with. That's a powerful feeling—to know that wherever you turn, you'll find offers of help to make your dreams come true.

Think big.

—Michael Port, *New York Times* bestselling author
of four books, including *Book Yourself Solid*
and *The Think Big Manifesto* and
founder of BookedSolidU.com

About the Author

Sharon Sayler, MBA, is a Communications Success Strategist and cofounder of Impression Engineers, an award-winning communication design and strategy company.

Sharon trains, counsels, and coaches professionals on how to become stronger, more influential communicators and leaders. She teaches people how to communicate with confidence and clarity by matching their verbals and nonverbals to create messages that produce successful outcomes.

Sharon combines her understanding of communications with a solid business background. She has served as a communication director for several companies and has owned a number of successful businesses. She considers herself a serial entrepreneur and an avid lifelong learner with practical, real-world application of nonverbal communication.

Sharon earned her MBA from George Fox University. She is an associate of Michael Grinder, one of the foremost authorities on nonverbal communication. She has contributed to several of Mr. Grinder's books, including *Charisma: The Art of Relationships*, published in 2004.

What Your Body Says is Sharon's third book. She is also the author of *Beyond Marketing: Building Relationships* and *Life's Short. Live Passionately*. A sought-after speaker, Sharon offers corporate trainings and seminars. For more information visit www.SharonSayler.com and www.WhatYourBodySays.com.

Acknowledgments

First and foremost, much love and appreciation to Adam and Jordan for showing me the true meaning of life. Mere words cannot begin to describe how eternally grateful I am to my sons, all my life-teachers, mentors, and friends I have met along the way. I have been blessed by many rich friendships, and each one has taught me to be more than what I was.

It is with love and gratitude that I thank all the people who have touched my life, not only those mentioned here who have shaped this book but also those who have inspired and encouraged me, so I am now able to know and use my gifts. I had no idea when I began this part of my journey how many people it takes to make an author. Thank you; I am forever grateful.

Thank you is too small for my mentors and friends for more than a decade, Michael and Gail Grinder. Thank you Michael Port, for believing in me and my message with your commitment, dedication, and high expectations. Thank you Dan Ambrosio, my editor, for your patience, guidance, and collaborative spirit. Thank you Lola Ready and Cara Lumen for teaching me how to express myself in the written word. Thank you Amy Ruppel, who took my words and made them real through her creative illustrations. In addition, much appreciation to my other heroes, too numerous to mention, who have spent hours reading and offering guidance as this book became real.

I wish to acknowledge and thank a special few who have made my life a grand adventure: my parents, Don and LaMae; my sisters, Linda and Janene; their husbands, Lowell and Michael; and my daughter-in-law Amanda. I thank those who have had a life-changing influence: Peter Bricca, Amethyst Susan Brown, Susan Byrd, Jim Dittmer, Vicki Joslyn, Megan McKenzie, Dave Parker, Stephen Parks, Don and Donna Pickens, Richard Quatier, Gerry Sayler, Joyce Sefton, and the cherished memory of Myrtle Madsen.

About This Book

What Your Body Says (and how to master the message) is more than a book, it is a guide to an approach to life. My hope is that it will help you understand through simple, nonverbal steps that you can add impact to your words and influence and inspire others to establish trust and build solid relationships. Every interaction with someone is a form of communication. If you've already had success in communicating, you've probably been using some of these techniques intuitively. However, consider the wide range of behavior options you'll have at your disposal once you become consciously aware of what you are doing. You will be the master of your own message—not the other way around.

Your individual success depends on what you do to prepare yourself for interactions with others. Developing an understanding of nonverbal communication allows you to choose from a wide range of actions. Not every technique works for everybody or every situation, and every situation is different. My aim is to provide you with enough new ways to look at communication so that when one approach isn't working, you have enough tools in your toolbox to try something else.

Warning: This is not a book about learning to read other people's body language. It focuses on being consciously aware of what messages your nonverbal cues are sending—the keyword here being **your**. Sure, most people are aware that arms across the chest mean someone is closing off their torso for some reason, a movement that might indicate that they are *closed* or maybe cold (or maybe they just have gas). You don't know the real reason because you're simply guessing. Quickly reading one movement or a single gesture of someone else's body language more accurately tells how they are feeling in the moment, not how they are thinking. If you had hours to spend observing someone's behavior, you might begin to understand what he or she is thinking. However, you would, at best, still be making an educated guess.

Therefore, in short, if you want to read minds, then this isn't the book for you. However, if you want to communicate with precision and clarity while inspiring others, you are in the right place. What you do with your body has a significant impact on how others perceive you. Once you use a few of the techniques in this book, you will never think about communication in the same way.

The methods presented in this book are simple to use and easy to remember. These strategies work best when you know *why* you are communicating. The *why* is the intention and the emotions behind the intention. Our unconscious nonverbal cues are aligned with our emotions, then our thoughts, then our words. Unless the *why* is brought to conscious awareness, the signals and cues associated with the emotions may send an unintended message of nervousness, apprehension, anticipation, or even ambivalence, even when using an appropriate gesture. When the *why* is brought to our attention, we can quickly and easily adapt our behaviors to send a different message.

Practice these techniques with the intention of conveying yourself clearly and creating lasting successful business relationships and you will succeed. Why? Because this works, all you have to do is use it. Learn the different approaches, adapt them to your unique situations, and practice every day. They will transform your communication success.

I can tell you from firsthand experience that learning this process changed my life. I was attending a workshop on non-verbal communication early in my training and while I knew what I was hearing was powerful, I had no idea why. Now I understand that the speaker's words and body language were sending the same message. He had the complete attention of all 50 members of the audience for more than 90 minutes before we took a coffee break. He walked up to me and whispered, "If you would think with your mouth closed, you would look more intelligent." I was astounded and hooked. Hence, I began my 12-year study into what my body says. I had no idea that my mouth had hung open while I listened in amazement. Lacking intelligence was certainly not the message I had intended to send. Find a mirror and let your jaw drop so your mouth hangs open. Not a very intelligent look, is it? Once I became aware of the emotional *why* (amazement), I adapted my behavior.

This is just one of the many discoveries you'll make as you explore your nonverbal cues, and the messages they send, through the pages of this book. The time you invest in increasing your familiarity and comfort with your own behaviors, and those of others, will pay you back repeatedly with genuine communication and lasting relationships.

Introduction

Have you ever walked away from a person, event, or situation and felt confused, and the experience made you feel uncomfortable and uncertain? You are not alone. Most likely, the subconscious cues—the nonverbals you saw—didn't match what you heard. So what to believe, your eyes or your ears?

If you are like most people, you believed your eyes, especially if you couldn't quite make sense of what you just heard.

Words are only a small part of communication. The most influential part of communication is your nonverbals. Your nonverbals can actually destroy or produce the results you want, such as inspiring employees to do better work, calming angry customers, creating fans in the marketplace, and closing sales.

Have you ever bought something you really didn't need—or hadn't intended to purchase—and later wondered, *Why did I buy that?* Most likely, it was because the salesperson saw nonverbal behaviors that let them know you were intrigued. The salesperson was looking for cues such as:

- One or both eyebrows raised.
- An upturn in the mouth.
- A slight sideways tip of the head.

1

- A lean in toward them (the salesperson) or the object of your desire.
- An audible *umm*.

As more of these nonverbal signals form a pattern, the salesperson knew with a high degree of certainty that with just a few more of the right words: *Bingo, they had a sale. They read you like a book.*

What if I told you that we all walk around with an *Owner's Manual* that everyone around us can read? That manual is full of nonverbal signals and cues about how we will behave, wish to be treated, and view others and ourselves. Problem is, most of us don't know what signals or cues we are sending. Most often we are not aware of what's in our own *Owner's Manual*, but everyone else is! That's why we are often treated differently than we expected.

In the About This Book section, I briefly described how the nonverbal signals and cues we send all the time can add impact to our words. Wouldn't it be nice to know which nonverbals can influence and inspire others and establish trust and build solid relationships?

The benefits of choosing your nonverbal communication are clear:

- To support what you are saying by complementing or adding to your verbal message. A manager with a palm up gesture is far more effective when complimenting an employee than one with a palm down gesture, since palm up matches the message *Good job!*
- To reinforce the verbal, use a visual aid to support the message. Oftentimes a message needs to be repeated if it's delivered only with words. If you use gestures, handouts,

flip charts, or other visual aids to support your message, the listener is not dependent on you alone for the message. Visual reminders allow listeners to process the information at their own speed.

- To emphasize or stress the importance of what is being said, either positively or negatively. A jump for joy or high-five will bring a different response than a foot stomp or eye-rolling.

On the other hand, nonverbal communication that contradicts your words can burden the listener with the task of sorting out mixed messages. Consider the statement "I'm fine" from someone whose nonverbals are shallow breathing, clenched jaw, narrowing of the eyes, and a dropped chin. These all lead the listener to believe the speaker is indeed not fine.

Depending on context, people might also send mixed messages when the nonverbal is the only communication. For example, you notice an interaction between a mother and young child. The mother has a raised eyebrow, direct eye contact with the child, a tip of the head, and a slight lean of the body toward the child. The mother is sending a message of delight or surprise. In a different context, the same set of behaviors could be sending the message, *No, don't do that*.

Recognize and remember that people communicate on many levels. Be aware of your own and observe others' facial expressions, eye contact, posture, hand and feet positioning, torso movement, and even how close or far away they are when they communicate. You want to use your nonverbals for communicating your feelings and what you're thinking by knowing:

- The positive intention of your message.
- The desired outcome.

- The context of your message.
- The content or what you want to say.

In this book, you will learn what I call intentional gestures, which when specifically chosen and consciously used, create the effect you want. The four intentional gesture categories are relationship (for conveying relationship between you and another person[s], or you and an object); location (for showing where things are located, including ideas and concepts); teaching (for instructing the listener on how to perform a task or understand a concept); and expectation or influence (for showing your own self-confidence and for managing another's behavior while leaving their self-esteem intact).

Since your physical gestures can silently change what you convey, why not have them transform your message by using intentional gestures? All too often a manager gets frustrated and resorts to power, for example saying, "I'm the manager, and I say so." Pointing a finger in someone's face should not be an option. There is no need to raise one's voice or shout each other down. Using intentional cues together with words increases the chances that your message will be understood the first time—without having to get frustrated or resort to power. Each verbal and nonverbal conversation either builds a relationship or destroys it.

We all know that communication is necessary to keep our personal connections strong and healthy. When everybody is on the same page, what we say can be a complete success. We all feel good about the interaction and achieving our goals. Other times, it can end in total disaster with hurt feelings, confusion, anger, and, worse yet, tears or ruined relationships. If positive relationship-based communication is to be at the heart of what we say, then we must realize that being a trusted, influential communicator requires a shift in thinking about how we view our verbal and nonverbal messages.

Consider this scenario: Once again, Amy was bent over her computer finishing the report that both she and Dick were supposed to give to the board of directors tomorrow. Dick had promised to finish it up, but instead said he had to do *research*. To Amy, the research looked like just playing around on the Internet. From his cubicle Dick yelled, "Hey, I'm hungry. What about getting something to eat? It sure would make it easier to finish up the report." The words had barely left his mouth before Amy was screaming, "This is your report too, why don't you ever work on it? And while you're at it, you go get the food for a change!" Dick was dumbfounded. "It was just a suggestion," he said. It probably was, but consider what Amy heard and didn't see. Dick was yelling to be heard across the cubicles. What Amy heard was Dick shouting and issuing a command. What she didn't see was that Dick's palm was turned up in a seeking gesture, his head was slightly tipped to the side, and he was smiling.

Too often the message heard differs from the message sent, especially when emotions are involved. How each person perceives the context of the message, the emotional state of both the listener and the speaker, and each person's intentions change the perception of the "rightness" or the "wrongness" of what is being said. As the example shows, both the speaker and the listener have their own unique filters that delete, distort, and generalize what was said and heard. Accepting that the original message may not have been received in the way it was intended is essential to keeping the lines of communication flowing, and to understanding intentional gestures and nonverbal influence.

EXERCISE: CLOSELY OBSERVE RESPONSES

Think of a recent conversation you had in which you felt it was important to get your point across. Did you get back the response you wanted? The response you got is a reflection of the message you sent. Record your recollection of the conversation.

- The Message I Thought I Sent
- The Response I Got
- The Response I Wanted

Your communication may not have succeeded because you were not clear about what you wanted to say, or your nonverbal communication was not as effective as you could have made it.

Understanding the Difference between Power, Intimidation, and Influence

Influence can be defined as the ability to get support from others to achieve an objective. Traditionally, the most common ways to influence are:

- Having a common purpose.
- Conditional—if you do this I will do that.
- Fear, which needs no explanation.

I would like to introduce another way: empowering others and showing them that you have complete confidence in their capabilities. Nonverbally this is achieved with gestures of expectation and influence. The true power behind influence is developed through relationships built on trust, confidence, and safety. Using the nonverbal cues of expectation and influence to support your message lets others know that you believe in them and they can do the work. The differences between influence to achieve an objective and influence to empower others can be overlaid—they are not mutually exclusive.

Each time you walk into the office, others can view you in one of three ways:

1. Who you are as the position you hold (the power you have).
2. Who you are as a person (a real human being with feelings).
3. A combination of the two (the ideal view).

Often our position affords us certain powers, which can be used to intimidate or enhance. For example, the office assistant who withholds critical information or stalls a project past the deadline is using power to intimidate. The office assistant who serves as a gatekeeper for her boss is using power to enhance the workflow.

There is nothing wrong with using power when needed. Decision makers are put in that position all the time. However, power carried to the extreme can be labeled intimidation.

By the same token, operating solely from the personal side can make it difficult to make decisions, especially if you want to be sure everyone is going to be okay before moving forward. Strive to stay in number three, the combination of the two.

How Influence Equals Opportunity

To be successful—and take an active part in building strong relationships—requires developing powerful spheres of influence. You can accomplish far more with others than alone. However, in order to build these kinds of connections, others must, of course, first know and like you. People do business with people they know, like, and trust, and avoid doing business with those they do not like. It's that simple. Are you friendly? Do you strive to make positive connections with others? Do you make and keep your commitments? These are examples of the questions people ask themselves when they meet you.

Although often wrong, the emotional part of the brain takes in the first impression and makes a snap judgment in an effort to understand what the person sees, hears, and feels by asking, *Do you care?* or *Why should I care?* or *Can I trust you?* It's the *Owner's Manual* again that answers these questions for them, through not only the words you choose but also your nonverbal cues, including:

- Tone of voice.
- Volume/speed of voice.
- Breathing.
- Expressions and gestures.
- Appearance.
- Posture and movement.

The nonverbal signals you send and receive can produce a wide range of responses, for example, intrigue, safety, trust, excitement, love, mistrust, apathy, fear, anger, or confusion. Unless you intentionally choose a nonverbal signal, you often don't know what signals or cues you are sending. Other people are never quite able to put their finger on why they like or dislike you. When asked, they'll answer, "I just know."

Hate to break it to you, but they got those answers from reading your *Owner's Manual*. The concept of the *Owner's Manual* answers the question of why the hardest worker or the most competent person in the room does not always win. It can be a tough lesson to learn. I know you've worked hard to be taken seriously. You earned the right letters after your name and then worked even harder to be seen as an expert at what you do. Then after doing it all right, nobody takes you seriously. Do you often have to repeat yourself or are you consistently being misunderstood?

Misunderstanding and miscommunication happen all the time. But why do they happen when everyone wants so badly to be understood? Could it be that your body language is sending a different message than you think it is?

What if, with a few simple changes, you could make each communication more effective? You can and this book will teach you how with skills based on nonverbal communication—the unspoken language. If you can become a master of the unspoken language and control your message, then you'll be able to inspire, influence, and build trust and strong relationships consistently.

Here's how it works. We all respond to nonverbal signals and cues. The instinct to use nonverbals is ingrained in our brains. Understanding these intuitive nonverbal behaviors is called emotional intelligence. Intentionally selecting nonverbals to enhance your message increases what we refer to as your **Influence Quotient.** The ability to build relationships and, in time, strong spheres of influence comes from being able to be understood quickly and easily. Nonverbal signals convey your message and the emotions behind your message more powerfully than words.

Your Influence Quotient is more important to your ultimate success than your intelligence quotient (IQ). Don't get me wrong, I am not disparaging intelligence. It is certainly important to approach everything you do with the mind of a learner to increase your knowledge at every opportunity. Yet even the smartest person in the room will have limited success if they can't influence others to work for and with them. Success doesn't happen in a vacuum.

In this book I have laid out an approach to master the message your body sends. Before we begin, here are three simple points to remember:

1. **There is some work involved.** At the beginning, you will be thinking about many options all at once, but that's okay. That is how you learn what works for you and what doesn't. The time you invest will be worth it, because the end product will be your ability to inspire, influence, build trust, and create lasting relationships.

2. **You will undergo a shift in perspective** and be able to see communication from three perspectives: yours, the listener's, and the observer's. There is nothing new here, really. You will simply tweak and change what you intentionally do and your perspective on how we all communicate and what is really being said.

3. **You can't go back.** I see it all the time. It's a lightbulb moment. The moment you use one of these techniques and immediately get the response you want, you will say, "Is it that easy?" Yes, it is. Once you integrate these insights into your toolbox of skills, you will never look at communication in the same way. This book will change the way you look at body language and nonverbal communication.

Items of Note

Most of the chapters have real-life examples to illustrate the topic. Some relate to the previous chapters and some do not. All details, including the names, have been changed to maintain the privacy and confidentiality of the work.

You may want to keep your responses to the exercises for review. I have prepared a complimentary *What Your Body Says Action Plan* with all the exercises in this book and more. Visit www.WhatYourBodySays.com to download your copy of the Action Plan so that you can begin today to master your body's message.

You will obtain great value from reading this book, yet the true values lies in your decision to implement what you learn. It is the implementation that will empower you to be a leader and achieve the communication success of which you know you are capable.

1 | The Signals You Are Sending

What Your Body Says (and how to master the message) explains the more commonly used nonverbal gestures and signals, which are easy to remember and duplicate without looking phony or forced. The primary focus is on body gestures, eye contact, and nonverbal cues of the spoken word—such as tone, volume, speed, and breathing. The goal is to learn to recognize the nonverbal behaviors, know how to apply them, and understand how they make others feel.

You are your nonverbals; they are a direct expression of your thoughts and emotions. Yet most people don't have a clue as to what they are expressing. It's simple to know what your body is saying, once you learn the language. This requires that you:

- First, observe others. Be curious, notice how their body language makes you feel so that you understand the most likely meaning of certain movements.

- Second, keep your sense of humor while you practice the skills in this book.

You likely choose your words very carefully, and explain each detail of a product or negotiation. But how often do you forget to choose what your body is saying? During a typical 10-minute conversation, a speaker and listener each send hundreds of nonverbal messages—that's a lot of messages, all of which have the potential to convey a mixture of meanings. Look at communication holistically:

- The words you say.
- The movements you make.
- The words the other person says.
- The movements he/she makes.

Communication comprises bits of messages and meanings—both verbal and nonverbal—that constantly travel back and forth. In life, as in poker, "He was so easy to read" means the other's nonverbal cues were sending messages loud and clear.

First impressions have a huge impact on how business relationships develop. If your nonverbal signals are not aligned with your words, people will more often believe what your body says—not your spoken words.

EXERCISE: CLOSELY OBSERVE GESTURES

Enjoy a conversation with friends and notice places you did or could have gestured. Write down a few examples to enhance your observation skills.

- The Words You Said
- Movements You Made

- The Words They Said
- Movements They Made

As you observe, begin to notice if there are shared gestures and movements. Look for ways to verify what you are seeing. You dramatically increase your ability to be an effective communicator when you become aware of nonverbal signals and cues. The basic techniques for sending nonverbal signals and cues are much the same for all professions. Whether you are designating tasks to be performed by employees, closing a sale, nailing the job interview, or presenting to a team, good communication skills are always an asset.

Good versus Bad Nonverbals

Behaviors and the patterns they create are neither good nor bad; they are simply behaviors. The context changes the perception of the rightness or wrongness of the behaviors. Every day we perform a balancing act between behaviors and patterns that are assets and those that are liabilities. Depending on the context, what might be a benefit in one situation may be a drawback in another. Imagine a sliding scale with assets on one end and liabilities on the other, and envision the following behaviors on that scale: raised voice, rapid breathing, stern tone, slightly dropped chin, erect posture, downward facing palm, and pointed finger. You probably placed these behaviors on the liability end of the scale, right? You might even label a person displaying those behaviors as upset or angry.

But consider this: by themselves, the majority of those behaviors do not indicate anger or distress. Each one plays a role, and in a different context might be used to alert others to danger. If someone were using those same reactions to keep us safe, we would consider them an asset. The context in which we use behaviors makes them a help or a hindrance. It is easy to select which behaviors to use in what context by keeping in mind the answers to these questions:

- What do my listeners want? What do I want?
- How do they get what they want? How do I get what I want?
- How can we both get what we want and maintain the relationship?

The key objective is to maintain the relationship while each person gets what he or she wants. Consider how you might do this with your own interactions.

EXERCISE: UNDERSTAND WANTS AND NEEDS

Think of an upcoming communication where your needs might vary from the listener's needs. Role-play that communication, and answer the following questions before you begin communicating with the other person(s).

What does my listener want?	What do I want?
How do they get what they want?	How do I get what I want?
How can we both get what we want and maintain the relationship?	

Understanding your needs and the needs of the listener is not a math question where the focus is on the value of each set of needs. The focus is on the relationship and how those needs can be met and if they can't be met, at least acknowledged. To understand needs, you must be willing to listen. Hearing is natural; listening is not. It takes concentration to listen effectively. To encourage others to share and show them that you are listening, use a downward glance and the head nod. The head nod is widely recognized to indicate approval or "Tell me more, I'm listening." The head nod goes up and down, differing from the side to side *no* headshake. Often the head nod and the headshake are behaviors we don't realize we are doing. That is why it is important to understand what messages our body is sending and intentionally choose behaviors that fit. Next time you want someone to share more, try a head nod and make eye contact with the floor for a while. The results might be surprising.

No one is born a great communicator, and no conclusive brain science exists to explain the difference between great and average communicators—except for learned behaviors often referred to as *charisma*. Great communicators use nonverbals intentionally, because they know it makes a difference in how others see them. Instead of spending their time learning to read another person's body language, great communicators work on how their body language is likely to be perceived.

As with almost everything else in life, anyone can learn to use nonverbal cues for clear communication. There are keys to being a successful communicator. It's not magic—it just looks that way.

2 | How the Signals Work

Since gesture is one of the words that usually come to mind when discussing nonverbal signals and cues, let's start there. A gesture is a movement or series of movements used to communicate a message. Now, that's a nice definition, but what does it really mean? Gestures and nonverbal movements or behaviors are part of who we are. Most often our movements are organic and spontaneous. Sometimes they represent what we are saying, and sometimes they don't. We often display emotions and thoughts nonverbally.

You want to be sensitive to the power that nonverbals have and deliberately choose those that support your message. Match your words with intentional gestures, those gestures made for a specific purpose. Nonverbal behaviors and groupings of behaviors, or patterns, when specifically chosen to correspond with your words, send an intentional message to the listener.

While hand gestures are the most common, any body movement can be an intentional gesture, such as rocking one foot on the tiptoe (unsure or coy), standing at attention with both feet

19

together (neutral or no comment), or having one or both feet turned toward the listener (interest in listener). Some research separates facial expressions from gestures; however, for simplicity's sake, I define gestures as any behavior or body movement, including those that involve the face.

Intentional Gestures Are a Powerful Tool

We all use gestures. We're just not always very good at having our gestures match what we say. Intentional gestures support your message and keep the listener fully engaged. They can also create an emotional response for both you and the listener. The emotional attachment to the message determines how the listener will respond.

Responding to gestures, especially smiles and other emotional facial expressions, is instinctive and cross-cultural. While members of all cultures respond to nonverbals, we don't necessarily do so in the same way, or consider them to have uniform meanings. For example, in North America, the okay gesture of the thumb and forefinger making a circle means everything is fine. In Japan, it means money; and in France, it means empty or zero. In Brazil and Russia, it can be an obscene gesture. Because of the cross-cultural issues, we will examine only the gestures that send the same intended message in most cultures. If you do a lot of international business, it's a good idea to study up on what is and isn't acceptable in various countries and across different societies. When in doubt, or if you don't understand what you see, just ask. The answer might surprise you.

Observe the local culture in different companies as well as countries. Each corporate culture, profession, or group has its own nonverbal gestures as well as jargon. It's impossible to know or write about all of them. However, by examining the four main types of gestures in *What Your Body Says,* you will be steps ahead in getting your point across. The four intentional gesture categories are:

- Relationship
- Location
- Teaching
- Expectation

There are countless gestures one can use to express elements of these four categories. Therefore, it's best to learn, practice, and adapt the basic ones. The best way to learn about gestures and their meanings is to practice a new one each day and observe how others react. Those that are presented here are combined to make patterns, so you can also practice one new pattern a week. The examples in this book show how intentional gestures can enhance the meaning and flow of what you are saying. Gestures can be used to replace the spoken word or utilized in conjunction with it. We use intentional gestures to emphasize the important parts of our message. This helps the listener know when to pay attention. After all, everyone's mind wanders, no one pays attention 100 percent of the time. You want to help the listener in any way you can by indicating the key points **you** want them to remember. There are two parts to an intentional gesture:

- The actual movement.
- The timing of the gesture.

The timing contains three elements:

- When the gesture happens (which word or phrase it accompanies).

- The length of time the gesture is in place (how long you hold the gesture).

- The intensity of the gesture (closer to your body or extended away from it, stiff or relaxed, one hand or two hands).

When and How the Gesture Happens

The brain typically sends gestures to your body at the same time you are formulating the words you want to say. When you are first learning to use intentional gestures, the brain formulates the words and then matches the gesture. As a result, your timing can appear to be somewhat off because the words and the gesture may not occur simultaneously. When you first start using intentional gestures, it is important that you know what you are going to say in advance. The timing of your gestures is a key skill to practice.

Avoid gestures that are random movements. Since gestures lose their effectiveness when they're out of sync with your verbal message, you want to coordinate your gestures with the words you're trying to emphasize. Pick the keywords or phrases to emphasize, based on your answers to the questions in Chapter 1:

- What do they want?
- What do I want?
- How do they get what they want?
- How do I get what I want?
- How do we both get what we want and maintain the relationship?

While it might seem like a lot to remember, working through the exercises and examples will allow you to see how easy it really is. Reinforce the listener's long-term memory by carefully timing your gestures so that they are in unison with the most important part of your message. The more you use intentional gestures, the more they become a habitual part of your natural nonverbal behaviors. For example, let's say that you are beginning the monthly team meeting by going over the agenda.

At a Glance		
"We need to cover five major points in today's meeting. Number one, we need to cover the sales report. Number two, we will review budgets. . . ."		
What Your Mouth Says	**What Your Body Does**	**The Message You Send**
We need to cover five major points in today's meeting.	Extend your arm straight from the shoulder, bending at the elbow to make an upward right angle. Show five fingers as you say the word *five*. Hold the gesture in place.	Pay attention, up here, folks. These five points are important.
Number one, we need to cover the sales report.	The gesture changes to indicate number one with one of your fingers going up.	Of first importance . . .
Number two, we will review budgets . . .	Have a second finger go up.	Next . . .

In this statement, *five major points* is the area to emphasize with a corresponding gesture that teaches. Use a gesture the audience is already familiar with to enhance clarity and comfort. Since you want the audience to remember *five*, hold up your arm to mimic the old right–turn signal. Then emphasize, **Number one, we need to cover the sales report**, with a gesture. (The gesture changes to indicate number one with one of your fingers going up.) **Number two, we will review budgets**. (Indicate with a second finger going up.) And so on.

The gestures add a visual reminder that often saves you from having to repeat yourself. A curious side effect of counting nonverbally is that the audience remembers which finger is the sales report and which finger is the budget. They often use the same fingers in recounting the message to someone else.

Using intentional gestures like counting to stress important points works for large audiences, small groups (eight or fewer), and one-to-one communication. You'll want to lessen the intensity of the gesture when speaking to eight or fewer people. To do this, simply make the gesture smaller or closer to your body. For example, when stating "We need to cover five major points in today's meeting," there is no need for the larger gesture of raising the arm. Simply raise your hand by bending only at the elbow, like a princess wave. (The counting on the fingers can remain the same.)

EXERCISE: PRACTICE TIMING YOUR GESTURES

Timing is important when using intentional gestures. Your goal is to have nonverbals and verbals match, since it is truly elegant when the two are in sync. Make sure you practice these and observe the responses. While most people are quite forgiving as you practice to get the timing exact, don't use their understanding as an excuse for letting your timing slide. You will discover the added benefit that people may not know why they like to listen to you; they just know that they do, because you are easy to understand.

How Long to Hold the Gesture

As your use of the intentional gesture becomes natural, add refinements, such as the length of time you hold the gesture. This will vary with the gesture's intention. To understand which length of time is appropriate for which gesture, let's review how a verbal message is delivered.

A verbal message has two parts: the actual spoken word and the silent pause between the segments, sentences, and thoughts. The silent pause allows the speaker to breathe. A silent, gestured pause allows the speaker to breathe and emphasize key parts of the message. Holding a gesture still (keep the same gesture, do not move it) throughout the pause allows the listener's mind to see, feel, interpret, and internalize the message, which adds more impact to the verbal message. The listener has the greatest opportunity to internalize the message during the speaker's pause. They are not busy listening to what else they might be missing at that time. The gestured pause allows the listener to catch up, comprehend and make correlations, and put the message in the proper place in memory. Move the gesture only when you begin to speak again.

"But Wait, There's More . . ." Connecting Two Ideas Nonverbally

Having the same gesture end a phrase and held still throughout the pause joins what was just said with what you will say next. Let's look at an example. Christine is smart, well-educated, and good at her job. She is friendly, well-liked, and easily develops rapport with customers and coworkers alike. Yet she often gets the sense that no one takes her seriously, even though she uses intentional gestures as she speaks. Christine claims that every time she starts to offer valuable contributions to the meeting, other attendees do not let her finish her point. Each time she stops to take a breath, they jump in and talk over her. Why? Because when she's speaking, Christine will make an intentional gesture, and then quickly drop it back to her lap while pausing to breathe. By completing her gesture, she is sending the unintended message, "I'm done with what I have to say."

A common nonverbal misunderstanding takes place when the speaker does not hold the gesture still throughout the length of the pause. Most often the speaker's gesture drops when they finish speaking, signaling to the listener, "I'm done." Holding an intentional gesture still throughout the pause signals that you are not finished talking. It conveys that there's more to come. Holding a gesture still in mid-air holds the audience's attention.

Move or change the gesture only when the next words come out of your mouth if you want to hold the floor or connect what you previously said to what you're about to say. The "But wait, there's more . . ." skill doesn't use just the gesture to send the message to wait. Rather, this is done through the length of time and the nonmovement of the gesture during the entire pause. Holding a silent, gestured pause a second or two longer than you normally would increases the anticipation of what is to come next. Be careful, therefore, not to release your gesture early. Releasing a gesture can be as dramatic as dropping your hands to your thighs with a thud, or as subtle as curling your fingers back to close your palm, as if you were milking a cow. Moving or changing the gesture during the pause signals you have completed the message. So in order to hold the floor, hold the gesture.

The gestured pause also sends the message that you are linking the last thing you said with the next thing you will say. Why would you want to do this? Because short-term memory is limited in most people, and it's hard to remember everything that is said in a meeting. Intentional gestures hold your message together both verbally and in the listener's memory. Research indicates that most people can remember five to nine threads of information for the short term. There is a reason that phone numbers are only seven digits. When you join similar concepts or parts of your message, short-term memory places them together on the same thread of information. For example, the following message is joining a personal compliment of individual talents with a request for cooperation.

At a Glance

"You each bring talent to this project. This project will give all of us an opportunity to learn from the best." This message has two parts: (1) "You each bring talent to this project." (2) "This project will give all of us an opportunity to learn from the best."

What Your Mouth Says	What Your Body Does	The Message You Send
You each . . .	Start your gesture at your chest. Hold out one arm for a small group, both arms for a large group. Gesture toward the audience with the palm up and open. Hold it in place.	We are all talented.
bring talent to this project.	Pause while still holding the same gesture. At the exact time you begin to speak after the pause, change the gesture by bringing it back to your chest.	AND I know we can do this.

To join the previous message with a request for cooperation:		
What Your Mouth Says	**What Your Body Does**	**The Message You Send**
This project will give all of us . . .	Gesture back toward the audience with your palms down. Pause and hold, with weight on both feet.	We are in this together and
an opportunity to learn from the best.	At the exact time you begin to speak after the pause, clasp your palms together and hold.	I expect you to behave.

How to Disconnect Two Ideas Nonverbally

When you want to separate two ideas or phrases, simply drop your last gesture as you begin the pause. An effective refinement is to move your body during the pause as well. Whether you shift in your chair or walk across the stage, the change in location will disconnect what was last said from what will be said next.

Why would you want to disconnect concepts? This is something you would do when switching from a negative, such as *dismal sales* or *budgets are slim this year,* to the positives of the individual talent and team opportunities. For example, let's say that you are in the middle of a meeting and you have to explain why the new budget will be small, yet you want the team to be on board for the new project.

At a Glance

"Due to the current dismal sales projections, the budget for this project will be X dollars. You each bring talent to this project. This project will give all of us an opportunity to learn from the best."

You want to disconnect part one of this message from part two. (1) "Due to the current sales projections, the budget for this project will be X dollars." (2) "You each bring talent to this project. This project...."

What Your Mouth Says	What Your Body Does	The Message You Send
Due to the current dismal sales projections, the budget for ...	Gesture with your palm down to a visual of the budget, calendar, or wall and hold the gesture.	It's not me; it's this visual I'm pointing at that is causing the small budget.
this project will be X dollars.	Drop your gesture, look to the floor and move your body to disconnect from "dismal sales projections."	Okay, we are done with that. Let's move on.

To nonverbally disconnect part one of this message from part two:		
What Your Mouth Says	**What Your Body Does**	**The Message You Send**
You each bring talent to this project. This project will give all of us. . . .	Bring your head up, face the audience, and gesture with a sideways palm. Pause and hold the gesture.	And I mean each one of you is talented—including myself.
an opportunity to learn from the best.	At the exact time you begin to speak after the pause, clasp your palms together and hold.	AND let's cooperate, we are in this together.

Dropping the gesture between statements, breaking eye contact by looking at the floor, and moving locations create a curious amnesia in the listener's mind about what was just said. The break in the action and move to a new location indicate that the next thing you say will be different. This is helpful to remember, especially when you have to deliver bad news or for occasions when you commit a verbal faux pas.

A common verbal faux pas is when the speaker opens with a joke that falls flat. It's rarely a good idea to open with a joke, but what do you do when you are met with the audience's silence? Plan A: Move a few steps to a new location in silence while looking down at the floor. At the new location, change your nonverbals: pop your head up, make eye contact with the audience, and smile. Observe the audience's reaction. Ask yourself, are they breathing low? Are they smiling? Do they appear comfortable? If the answer is yes, continue with your presentation as if nothing happened.

Plan B: If the audience is breathing high, looking at each other or appears shocked or confused, you'd better do something because you're in deep doo-doo. First, keep breathing low. Move to a new location. Use the arm closest to the old location, which is contaminated from the joke that fell flat or the misunderstanding. Gesture toward the audience with the palm of your hand sideways and then begin to move your arm back toward the old location. While you are moving your arm, turn your forearm over so that your palm faces down. To keep their attention on where you are gesturing, look at your thumb. The audience will follow your eyes before they will follow your gesture. Keep your eyes on your thumb as you move your arm in the direction of the old location. Keep your eyes on your hand and shake your head *no* a couple of times, in silence. Without taking your eyes off your hand, drop your arm and head at the same time so that both your fingers and your eyes are pointing toward the floor. Move from that location in silence and pop your head up and smile. Continue as if nothing happened. You don't have to say anything. Shaking your head *no* resets the stage.

If all else fails and you believe the audience needs to hear about what just happened, poke fun at yourself in the third-person, as if you can't believe that person who was over there just said what he said. In the new location, use a friendly voice and say something, such as "I can't believe that guy opened with a joke." This is called a reframe. Reframing maintains the original content, but helps the audience look at it in a more open-minded and hopeful way. After the reframe, look down, walk to a new location in silence, pop your head up to make eye contact with the audience, smile, and start fresh. Often the nonverbal is more important than the verbal. Looking down and walking break the action, which provides time for any discomfort to dissipate. Who would have thought that by just looking down and moving, you could create a momentary amnesia in the listener? And the movement helps you recover.

These three concepts—timing, connection, and disconnection—are simple yet profound. You will see as you read further that there are more refinements to add to these techniques in order to increase your skills. For now, be consistent as you practice. Inconsistency confuses people. Knowing the complete message you want to send before you begin allows you to fine-tune the timing of your gestures and create the connection or disconnection of your message. These simple tools align you with your message, and are an essential part of creating trust with the listener. Trust is the essential element in building lasting relationships.

3 | Gestures of Relationship

Gestures of relationship have more flexibility than gestures of location, teaching, or expectation. The most common relationship gestures in a business setting are hand gestures; for example, the palm up, the palm down, and the sideways palm. A palm(s) up gesture is interpreted as friendly because it conveys that the speaker is open to suggestions and/or seeking information. You may have noticed that when asking questions, speakers often gesture with the palm up toward the other person. This makes others feel they are the center of attention. If the speaker and the listener already have a solid relationship, the palm facing up can also mean the listener is being called on to do something or respond in some way.

All gestures must be viewed in context. A palm facing up makes a person feel good, appreciated, listened to, or encouraged, while a palm facing down can stop two-way communication, and often makes others feel as if they aren't being heard. The palm(s) down gesture says you are sending information, or this topic is very serious and/or not open to discussion. The palm(s) sideways gesture means you are discussing something serious or are on the fence about the issue.

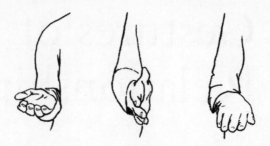

There is a gender bias for the palm sideways gesture, which is midway between the openness of the palm up and the closed feeling of the palm down. Women from Western cultures rarely use the palm down gesture. When a woman uses the palm sideways gesture, she usually means the same thing that a man means when he uses a palm down gesture—that this is serious and/or is not open to discussion. If you want to express that something is serious or sensitive or not open to negotiation, use the palms down gesture. This can be interpreted as friendly, but serious, if it is done with a smile and comfortable eye contact. However, depending on context, it may be read as a power gesture.

Both positive and negative gestures can be used to build or damage a relationship, depending on the context and your intention. Sometimes a leader uses a gesture with a downward open palm to say, "My mind is made up" and that's okay. The negative gesture of relationship is not necessarily bad, it is simply the opposite of positive. Other relationship gestures include a tip of the head, a handshake, toes pointed toward the listener, and, of course, the smile. These all come naturally and are easy to use. Hand gestures should be performed smoothly and steadily with an even flow.

EXERCISE: PRACTICE GESTURES
OF RELATIONSHIP

Try this: Hold your forearm parallel to the ground, close to your waist. At a steady pace, move your hand and arm away from your waist out to a 90–degree angle and back to your waist. Smooth and steady, it's that easy. This positive gesture of relationship looks natural and fosters the personal side of the relationship. Try it with an open palm facing up, an open palm sideways, and the open palm facing down. Notice how each position makes you feel. Ask a friend to do the same exercise. Have your friend gesture toward you in the same way. Notice how each position makes you feel. Ask your friend how it felt.

The amplification of a hand gesture is determined by the size and context of the group to which one is speaking. Two-handed gestures add more emphasis than one-handed gestures. With both one- and two-handed gestures, the straighter the elbow the stronger the emphasis. One-handed gestures are better for one-to-one relationships, when seated, or in small groups of eight or fewer people. They typically begin at the elbow and use a comfortable flowing movement of the forearm. Two-handed gestures can begin at the shoulder and use the whole arm and hand to amplify the size of the gesture by positioning the arm to flow from the shoulder. Using both hands allows for greater visibility of the gesture for large groups.

Intentional gestures are not about looking choreographed, phony, or forced. They are about supporting the intention of the message. For example, if you are delivering positive or good news, gesture back and forth between yourself and the listener(s) with an up-facing, open palm. Positive news can be anything that is not negative, such as the neutral statement, "The weather is fine." On the other hand, good news would be, "The boss loved the report we wrote." Use an up-facing, open palm gesture for both the fine weather and the report.

Herb, a bartender at a local restaurant, often has people waiting for a seat at the bar even though tables are open. He makes more tips than any of the servers. When asked about the secret of his loyal following, Herb claims that he tries to make everybody who comes his way feel good about themselves. Management and staff watched him for days, but never heard or saw him say or do anything unusual. He merely talked about the weather or some positive news in the paper that day. Others tried doing the same but without success. Finally, Herb shared his secret. Each time he said a positive word about whatever he was talking about, he gestured toward his listener with an upward open palm and casually returned the gesture toward himself. Thereby, he was connecting himself and his listener to the positive words with gestures of relationship. Start with a statement that contains a positive word, such as "It's a **wonderful** day!"

Remember, intentional gestures emphasize words or topics of importance. The key word in this example is *wonderful*. Herb gestures toward the listener as he starts the positive word, thereby assigning the virtues of wonderful to the listener. By flowing the gesture back toward himself as Herb ends the word *wonderful*, he acknowledges to the listener that the listener, Herb, and wonderful are joined. This technique is effectively used during introductions to create a positive first impression.

At a Glance		
A positive opening between two people. "It's a wonderful day, the weather is perfect!"		
What Your Mouth Says	**What Your Body Does**	**The Message You Send**
It's a wonderful day, . . .	One arm starts at the center of your chest and makes a sweeping movement out with an open palm to the listener. Arm moves gently back toward yourself.	We are both wonderful.
the weather is perfect!	Hold the gesture by moving arm slowly back and forth between yourself and the listener while you finish the sentence and linger on the word *p e rf e c t*.	We are both perfect.

To display a higher degree of interest, you can refine a positive gesture of relationship to let others know that you agree, are interested, or want to belong by slightly leaning toward them or the object of your interest.

Leaning increases the level of commitment to the relationship. Your interest can be displayed by the degree of lean and where you place your body: to the side or face to face. The face-to-face position exposes the entire body, putting the body in a vulnerable position. This position conveys a high degree of interest and a feeling of safety. Obviously, you can't lean too much without falling over, yet a slight forward jutting of the head says, "I'm listening intently," while a lean from the waist or ankles displays greater interest. The lean should be slight and not be a lunge. You always want to respect others' comfort zones and personal space.

At a Glance		
A positive opening to a large group.		
"It is so great to join you today. Isn't it a wonderful day!"		

What Your Mouth Says	**What Your Body Does**	**The Message You Send**
It is so great to join you today.	Both arms start at the center of your chest and then make a sweeping movement out wide. Both palms are open and turned upward as you hold this gesture toward the audience.	We are all great.
Isn't it a wonderful day!	Hold the gesture still while you linger on the word *w o n d e r f u l.*	We are all wonderful.

The larger the audience, the more dramatic the gesture and the longer you can linger on the positive words. In large groups, start the gesture at your shoulder(s).

At a Glance

Conveying positives to a large audience throughout your message.

"Sales are doing **great** this quarter. We are looking forward to next quarter being one of the **best** yet."

What Your Mouth Says	What Your Body Does	The Message You Send
Sales are doing **great** this quarter.	With both arms starting at the center of your chest, make a sweeping movement out and open to encompass the entire audience. Both palms are open and turned upward as you say the word *great*. Hold this gesture toward the audience. Pause while still holding the same gesture. At the exact time you begin to speak after the pause, move your arms back to your chest.	We are all great and in this together. I sincerely mean what I am about to say next. We are in this together, so let's cooperate.
We are looking forward to next quarter being one of the **best** yet.	With both arms starting at the center of your chest, make a sweeping movement out and open to encompass the entire audience. Both palms are open and turned up or sideways as you hold this gesture toward the audience.	We are all the best.

There are a few hand gestures that do not build relationships, and can even deter our interactions with others. I strongly suggest everyone stay away from the pointed, often bouncing index-finger gesture, the one that looks like a chicken pecking. This can feel like a personal attack, especially when discussing negatives.

A variation of the index-finger point is the steeple point. It is an extension of the steeple gesture. The steeple gesture, to be used without pointing the fingers at someone, most often implies, "I'm an expert" or "I'm comfortable with what I know." The steeple point is the same gesture except the speaker tips the fingers from pointing up like a steeple to pointing at the listener. While this gesture is used for sending information, it often does not send the intended message. Instead, it sends the message, "I'm an expert, and I want you to know I'm the expert here." To create a steeple point, place your hands together without touching palms, thumbs pointed up, fingers directed forward. Touch only the fingertips and thumb tips. Palms should not touch, and fingertips face the audience. Often, the speaker bounces the steeple point in time to the important points they are sending. The pointed fingers aimed at the audience along with a bounce timed to the key points *hits* the listener with every bit of information the speaker just said. Using this gesture when you present bad news assigns various parts of the bad news to the audience. Assigning a negative to the listener, especially with the steeple point, definitely hurts the speaker's likeability factor.

Be careful where you assign or aim your gestures. Not only will you make the listener feel bad by pointing and saying negative words to them, but they will associate you with the negative words as well. If you are not careful, they will view you as negative and part of the problem.

How to Attach Yourself to a Message

To attach yourself to your message, start with your palms over your chest. If you want to increase the emotional intensity of your message, start with your palms over your heart. Then extend both arms out toward the audience, palms up as you say the words you want to be connected with. As you finish the statement, fold your arms back to have your palms cover your chest (or heart) once again.

For example, everyone loves the new company mission statement. You want your audience to see you as part of that positive feeling about the company and its new mission.

At a Glance

"Our company is committed to delivering services based on superior industry knowledge, real understanding of the issues, and a genuine enthusiasm for what we do."

What Your Mouth Says	What Your Body Does	The Message You Send
Our company is committed to delivering services based on superior industry knowledge, . . .	Start at your heart, palms facing your chest. Hold gesture.	I'm committed to this. I have superior industry knowledge.
real understanding of the issues, and . . .	Sweeping two-arm gesture with palms up and open toward the audience. Hold gesture toward audience.	We all have a real understanding of the issues.
genuine enthusiasm for what we do.	Bring gesture back to your heart, palms flat as if to cover your heart and hold until the end of this statement.	And I, the speaker, have a real understanding and enthusiasm.

If you really want to attach yourself to the positive aspects of a message, use an object that represents the positive and hold it to your chest as you gesture or create a visual placeholder for the message. Politics and religion aside, think TV preacher here. Have you ever wondered why they gesture to the sky and back to themselves or hold icons so tightly to their chest? They are nonverbally cementing themselves, the locations, and the visual reminders together in the mind of the listener. It is easy to inadvertently connect yourself to a message. Always be careful with the connection gesture pattern, make sure it is a message you want to be connected with.

How to Create a Visual Placeholder

Since it's that easy to attach yourself to a message, what happens if you have bad news and don't want to be stuck to it? Worse yet, how do you move a message you are inadvertently connected with? One way to detach yourself is to use an object or phantom location as a visual placeholder to hold the news (which is usually bad news), and aim your gestures at the placeholder. The placeholder becomes the bearer of the bad news. Speak of the placeholder in third-person, such as "On the flip chart you will see. . . ."

Even though many claim that we shouldn't *shoot the messenger,* we all do to some extent. Remember, if you're discussing a negative topic, gestures of relationship between you and the listener will place this negativity on the listener or yourself. You probably don't want to be known as the bearer of unpleasant or bad news. Your goal is to transfer the negative onto an object or visual placeholder. Be careful not to use gestures of relationship between a negative visual placeholder and you or the listener. End the gesture to the placeholder by dropping the arm straight down. An elegant refinement is to drop your head and look down at the arm you just dropped at the same time, thereby disconnecting both your eye contact and gesture from the placeholder.

Most often, it does not motivate a team to go sell more when words such as disappointing (as in *disappointing sales*), or way down (as in *profits are way down*) are assigned to the team instead of the visual placeholder. Let's say that you have to report disappointing sales and profits, along with the optimistic news that sales are projected to go up.

At a Glance

Have the visual placeholder, such as a flip chart, on a stand set off to the side before you begin to speak.

"It is unfortunate to report the company had disappointing sales this season. Profits are way down. On the brighter side, sales are projected. . . ."

Hint: Speak in third-person about negatives.

What Your Mouth Says	What Your Body Does	The Message You Send
It is unfortunate to report the company had disappointing . . .	Extend your arm with your palm sideways and direct eye contact to the visual placeholder. Hold the gesture and eye contact.	That visual placeholder caused this disappointment, not me.
sales this season. Profits are way down.	Move the gesture to the location on the placeholder that references profits. Drop the gesture straight down to your side; do not bring the arm back to your waist. Move your head to look down at the floor while maintaining a silent pause; breathe and move to a new location.	This is not good either. It's not me, I didn't cause this. I am separating myself from this bad news.
On the brighter side, sales are projected. . . .	At the new location, quickly pop your head up, make eye contact, smile and gesture with palms up.	We are moving on. We have amnesia for what was just said. I'm excited, let's get on with this.

Place news that is anything less than positive at a location that does not relate to you or the listener. Aim the gestures off to the side, and remember context and intention. It works far better to build quality relationships and empower others by nonverbally assigning positive words to people, and negatives to places or objects.

Here is a scenario: You have to deliver a report to the board of directors with the news that profits are way down. Of course, the last thing you want the board to think is that you're the reason for this bad news.

At a Glance

Have the visual placeholder, such as a flip chart, on a stand set off to the side before you begin to speak.

"As you can see, the report states that profits were down 21 percent for the last quarter, compared to 18 percent in the previous quarter. It is projected that profits will continue to remain. . . ."

Hint: Speak in third-person about negatives.

What Your Mouth Says	What Your Body Does	The Message You Send
As you can see, . . .	Make eye contact with the audience. Extend the arm closest to the visual toward the audience, with your palm sideways, arm slightly bent. Watch your thumb as you move your arm so that your eyes and arm move in unison. This will guide the audience to the visual. As you guide the audience's eyes, straighten your arm, roll the forearm to allow for a palm down gesture as you arrive at the visual. Don't lock the elbow. As you reach the visual, the palm should be down. Hold gesture.	[With the visual in place] Look, it's not me! It's that visual over here that has bad news.

the report states that profits were down 21 percent for the last quarter . . .	While keeping your palm down, move your arm to correspond with the 21 percent point on the visual. Hold gesture.	Shame on that bad quarter.
compared to 18 percent the quarter before. It is projected that profits will continue to remain . . .	While keeping your palm down, move your arm to correspond with the 18 percent point on the visual. Hold each gesture in place. When examination of the data is complete, maintain a silent pause longer than normal to breathe and allow the audience to breathe, since negative news does take the breath away. Look down and drop arm straight to your side at the same time, and then step away one or two paces. Continue looking down, pause and breathe. Move from that location.	Shame on this bad quarter too. I didn't want to have to tell you this. . . .

If you are not sure how your audience is going to receive certain news, such as the report you wrote, and you cannot create a larger visual placeholder for the bad news, hold the report off to the side, and use words such as "the report says" instead of "my report." Using third-person language deflects the negative onto the object and does not connect it to you. Once the boss announces that he loves the report, enthusiastically clutch it to your chest and proclaim it as your own.

A visual placeholder can be anything. It can be a drawing, words on a flip chart, a computer presentation, a handout, a phantom location, or even a story that paints a picture that listeners can remember visually. And the placeholder can hold anything that represents what you are talking about, whether it is good or bad.

While props like flip charts and posters may seem old-fashioned, I strongly encourage you to use visual reminders like these. They can be prepared in advance or written on the spot, and they create a permanent visual record to remember, which helps boost long-term memory. When you're giving a presentation that involves several pages, post the pages you want the audience to remember around the room. (If the meeting is two days or more, keep each visual in the exact same location.) An added benefit of flip charts or posters is that they can be hung up back at the office, or photographed and shared. When I give presentations, I photograph the posters after the event and post them on a blog for participants to refer to later.

You can also provide a consistent look for a visual using a computer presentation template. While this is useful for news that needs to be precise, such as charts and graphs, it is not very good for long-term memory retention and can actually impede attention unless done correctly. It can also replace you and become the star of the event. Using this type of presentation puts you at risk for becoming a sound track for your slides.

If handled correctly, handouts can be valuable tools. They aid understanding of detailed or complicated material. Nevertheless, they can also be a distraction. Some tips to minimize this unwelcome side effect:

- Hold up the handout at the beginning of the presentation and tell your listeners that they will receive a complete version at the end.

- If handouts are needed during the meeting, distribute sections at each point necessary to keep the audience on task.

- If you use a workbook, color-code the sections, and show the code system before you begin. When it comes time to examine a section, hold up the corresponding color.

- Include places to take notes and fill in blanks. Some members of the audience like the muscle memory created by filling in blanks.

- When giving directions verbally on how to use the handouts, use the words that set the audience in motion last. "The answers are on page 12" is preferable to "Page 12 has the answers." As soon as the audience hears *page 12,* they start moving and stop listening to you.

As mentioned previously, a visual placeholder does not have to be a physical object. It can be constructed through gesture and words. If you create a mind's eye picture or phantom location, others will believe it is real. In order to do this, think like a mime. Gesture to that specific location as if what you told the audience was there actually is there. (A more detailed explanation of this process can be found in Chapter 4, the section entitled How to Create a Phantom Location.)

Sometimes a story and/or metaphor with intentional gestures will work better than an actual visual placeholder when conveying positives to your audience. Stories can offer meaning and context that reflect the world we live in, and provide a new way to look at reality. For example, consider the sentence, "The brave warriors marched over the mountain to view the lovely sunrise." By gesturing toward the audience as you say the words *brave* and *lovely*, your audience will perceive that you called them both brave and lovely.

Whether in metaphor or reality, say and show your audience that you appreciate them and that you care about their feelings. Be engaged, you must connect with your message for the audience to connect. If you can't seem to do so, then reexamine the intention and your emotions behind the message. A client once said, "Who cares about all this? Shouldn't they know I like them?" Why should they know? If you want to leave a lasting impression, leave them feeling self-confident, capable, and good about themselves and you.

4 | Gestures of Location

You've probably already noticed how intentional gestures can relate, overlap, and build on each other. The previous chapter left your audience feeling self-confident, capable, and good. You learned to create a visual placeholder to draw the audience's attention to a new location. Locations allow us to maintain and build on the positive feelings we create with our gestures of relationship. Here we take the concept further to understand how to maintain those positive feelings, even when we have not-so-positive information to share, by understanding phantom locations. There are four directions for gestures of location:

1. Toward yourself [positive].
2. Toward the listener [positive].
3. Within the immediate vicinity—next to you, on the floor, or on a visual such as a flip chart [negative].
4. Outside the immediate vicinity—out a window, the far corner, way over there [negative].

Each of these four locations comes in handy when given a context and an intention.

How to Use Locations

In terms of speaking to others, **locations** are as follows: you are one, the listener is another, and there are two neutral locations—within and outside the immediate vicinity. As often as possible, you'll want to assign good news to the locations of yourself and the listener. This enhances the positive feelings of relationship and connection. Connect negatives to yourself or the listener only when you have a specific context/reason.

Consider possible outcomes carefully before assigning a negative to a person. Once a negative is placed with a person, if left unresolved, it can create an uncomfortable feeling, not only for the person to whom it was assigned, but also for those who saw and felt it being assigned. The need for resolution can create a sense of emotional urgency for the person and/or witnesses to take action. It can also cause resentment and hurt feelings.

For example, if you gesture to a person when you are upset or angry, you are nonverbally assigning those feelings and actions to that person. Try to recall a time when a friend told you something upsetting that happened to him and aimed his upset gestures toward you. Those negative feelings were nonverbally assigned to you—even though your friend likely did not intend them to be.

At a Glance		
"John, I can't believe what happened to me on the freeway. Some jerk cut me off. I got so mad I gave him the one-finger salute."		
What Was Said to John	**What the Friend's Body Said**	**The Message the Friend Sent**
John, I can't believe what happened to me on the freeway. Some jerk cut me off.	The friend begins to gesture toward John with a rigid forearm, moving it up and down quickly in a hatchet fashion, the fingers pointed directly at John. The gesture stops as he releases his frustration.	John's friend just nonverbally called him a jerk and gave him the one-finger salute. How would you feel? Most people feel crummy, yet can't tell you why. After all, his friend was only relaying a story.
I got so mad, I gave him . . .	The gestures start up again and this time he includes direct eye contact.	
the one-finger salute.	He makes the gesture at John to show him what he did to the other driver.	

Think how often this happens in relationships, for example, when you complain to a boss or coworker and then wonder why they cringe when they see you coming. In turn, the listener wonders why they feel so bad when you are done. You feel so much better because you have gotten it off your chest, but you have literally placed it on theirs. Think about the implications of conveying negative feelings through gestures toward a loved one (and we wonder why they aren't always overjoyed to see us each night when we come home from work!).

Negative attributes have a longer afterlife in short-term memory than positives do. The memory quickly files the positives away, because they are complete. There is nothing left to resolve or figure out. However, working with negatives is not a comfortable state for the short-term memory. It desires resolution—either into a positive or at least a lesson learned before the memory can comfortably store the negative and move on.

Consider yourself one location and the listener another and predetermine possible alternate locations within a larger area to gesture toward when referring to negatives or bad news. Choosing a gesture location in advance is important, because negatives have a way of contaminating the things and people with which they come in contact. Assign negatives to a visual placeholder or phantom (neutral) location as often as possible. A location within the immediate vicinity creates a sense of urgency and emotional impact more than one outside the immediate vicinity. It is much easier to decontaminate or ignore a phantom location than yourself or another person.

How to Create a Phantom Location

A phantom location is an ideal placeholder for negatives. Phantom locations are neutral spots that can be quickly created and from which you and your audience can easily be disassociated. Try to think like a mime when you're choosing a phantom location. How does a mime make you believe he is behind a wall? He implies that there is a wall by using exaggerated gestures. This same concept holds true here. As you begin to talk about something that does not have a visual placeholder for the listener, gesture toward a predetermined location either beside you, behind you, in a corner, or even out the window. Remember, the closer it is to you or the listener, the more emotional attachment and sense of urgency to resolve.

If you act as if a phantom object or concept were really at a given location, others will believe it is there too. It is a curious phenomenon. You can assign anything you want to a location, even something as abstract as bad news. Although listeners are not able to see an object or concept physically, such as bad news piled up in the corner, they will believe it is there if you consistently reinforce that it is. The key here is to maintain the same location and gesture for whatever you originally placed there, especially if it's negative news.

How to Assign Negatives to a Location

Keep the primary presentation location from being contaminated. Remember to use hand gestures to place topics that could be controversial in phantom locations. For example, you have assigned questions and answers (Q&A) to the right corner of the room through a previous hand gesture while saying that you will be taking Q&A at the end of the presentation. Walk to that location before you answer any questions. While Q&A may seem like part of your primary presentation, it is too easy to be surprised by a question or led down a tangential path that can muddle the primary message.

The practice of preserving the primary presentation location makes the visual placeholder or phantom location, not you, the bad guy. Of course, you don't want to announce overtly to the audience that you are going to give them bad news at that spot over there. That's just weird and unnatural. To assign a bad news location, first establish nonverbally that you use locations. You can do this by beginning your presentation in the primary location with "Welcome, thank you for attending. The topic today is . . . ." Take a few steps toward the predetermined location where you will deliver bad news. With a gesture toward the new location, begin to explain why you are moving. For example, "Before we begin, we will review the disappointing sales report." At the new location—where it's best to already have set up a visual placeholder like a flip chart—deliver the bad news.

At a Glance

"Before we begin, we will review the disappointing sales report. Some of us may be concerned about. . . ."

What Your Mouth Says	What Your Body Does	The Message You Send
Before we begin, we will review the disappointing sales report.	Move from the primary presentation space toward the location where you are placing the "disappointing sales." Once you step away from the primary location, extend your arm with your palm sideways to the bad news location (for example, the corner to your left) within the room. Remember this location.	The flip chart and those people who didn't buy anything are over there, where I am pointing. They caused this; I didn't.
Some of us may be concerned about . . ."	At the new location, extend the arm closest to the visual placeholder with a gesture toward it. Place palm sideways to express concern or palm down for serious concern. Bring your other hand up to your chest.	I can't speak for all of you, but this is something I myself am concerned about.

Conclude that part of your presentation. Look down and drop the gesture. Do not return it to your torso at the same time. Pause and remain still for a moment. In silence, continue looking down as you move to a new location. At the new location, bring up your head and eyes, make eye contact with the audience, and start with a new topic.

Choose a bad news location that is one you would not walk through in the normal course of your presentation, such as the far end of the stage, a corner, the back of the room, or even the opposite side of the flip chart. When you have completed the bad news, you will want to disconnect yourself from the bad news location. Remember the nonverbal way to disconnect two ideas? You can do the same in regard to a location by simply dropping your head/eyes and your last gesture as you begin your pause, and then silently changing location. Whether you shift in your chair or walk across the stage, the silence, dropped gesture, and change in location will detach your last statement from what you are introducing next. If you are unable to change locations, shifting nonverbals, such as taking off your glasses, will accomplish the same thing. Changing location or nonverbals leaves the bad news *over there*.

Assigning a phantom location for a topic, especially one that is unpleasant for most people to hear about, works because of the way our memory operates. Have you ever walked into a room and wondered what you came in for, only to go back to the original location and remember exactly why you went to the other room? The visual reminder of the first room jogged your memory. Visuals, location, and memory are connected. For instance, when they are driving, many people replay directions in their mind's eye, such as "Turn right at the big oak tree." They have assigned the directions a visual reminder of location.

In the example from Chapter 3, Gestures of Relationship, where you have to report the negative (disappointing sales and profits down) along with the positive (sales are projected to go up), the first gesture is to place your palm sideways pointing over there—away from the listener—to where disappointing sales happen. That assigns the disappointment to a location outside your vicinity. As you might guess, the farther away you assign the location, the less urgency the audience feels to deal with the bad news. Politics aside, consider TV stations' coverage of war to understand the concept of location, urgency, and emotional attachment. Even though you hear about a war, it is still far away. It is the visual of TV that creates the urgency, emotional attachment, and memory.

Let's say that you want the audience to know the facts, but not feel an emotional urgency to resolve the negative. Place the negative far away.

At a Glance		
"It's unfortunate to report we had disappointing sales this season. Profits are way down. On the brighter side, sales are projected...."		
What Your Mouth Says	**What Your Body Does**	**The Message You Send**
It's unfortunate to report we had disappointing ...	With arm straight and palm down, point out the window where sales happen. If there's no window, gesture with the palm down to an outside wall. Bounce the arm once or twice.	Out there is where it's disappointing.
sales this season. Profits are way down.	Hold the gesture as you finish the word *down*, look down at the same time you drop the arm straight down—do not return the gesture to yourself (your chest or thighs). Returning the gesture directly to your body will attach the negative to you. Change locations in silence.	It's not my fault; I have no part of it.
On the brighter side, sales are projected ...	Pop head up, make eye contact with the audience, and smile. Start at your chest and extend both arms toward audience with a wide gesture, palms up.	Brighter days are ahead.

If, on the other hand, you want to create strong emotions and encourage the audience to *feel the pain,* you can use your gestures to place the bad news in front of the audience. However, I do not normally recommend this gesture. While you will create a strong reaction with this move, you won't be a hero. If you do choose this solution, it shouldn't be based on how you feel, but rather on what the group needs. This technique is often used when the group is highly dysfunctional, and the speaker has decided to switch from managing to disciplining the group.

To successfully have the audience feel the pain and maintain the relationship afterwards, you must breathe low and comfortably while making eye contact with limited blinks. Once the nonverbal behavior pattern is complete, and you have gained compliance, drop the gesture, pause, breathe, and in silence, immediately move from that location, as it is now contaminated by the negative news and the power gesture. Remember, you placed the bad news between you and the audience. As you move, look down, stay silent, and continue to breathe low and slow. When you arrive at the new location, look up, make eye contact, stay silent for a moment, and start fresh with new nonverbals. If you choose this method, offer a strong positive reframe or solution so that you are seen as part of the solution, not the problem.

Example: [Breathe low.] "It is unfortunate to report that we had disappointing ... [Start with arms at sides at the bad news location. Do not bring this gesture from your waist or chest. Bring both arms straight up and out with your palms sideways to the audience.] ... sales this season. Profits are way down." As you move through this gesture, roll your arms from the shoulder to turn your palms down. Aim the gesture to the space between you and the audience. Hold the gesture and pause slightly longer than normal, while continuing to breathe low. Look down at the same time you drop the arms straight down. Do not return the gesture to you, your chest, or thighs. Continue looking down as you change locations in silence. The message you sent is "Hey, people, you are disappointing."

How to Avoid Cross-Contaminating Your Message

Don't cross-contaminate your message, yourself, other people, or other locations in the room. Once you have assigned topics to various locations, remember where they are. Choose locations to move to based on the sensitivity of the topic and the way you normally move when you speak. For instance, most right-handed speakers move more often to the right than they do to the left. They should choose a location for bad news to their left, as the likelihood of accidentally wandering through that location is less. Bad news travels, and it is possible to nonverbally drag the bad news from its location to other parts of the room. This may sound unusual, but it really does happen and it is just like getting toilet paper stuck to your shoe.

Contamination occurs when the negatives are not left in the location that you chose for them. Leave negatives where you placed them by dropping the previous gesture down toward the floor instead of returning the gesture to your torso.

Changing location to leave the bad news over there is Plan A when you want to disconnect and decontaminate one part of your message from the previous part. Having multiple locations is a proactive choice that works well to keep your primary location from being contaminated. However, the silent change of location only works to separate the two parts in the memory of the listener when the violation is small, for example, an occasion when an attempt at humor or an answer regarding a controversial subject is not well received.

For larger violations, enhance the separation by changing location and the majority of your nonverbals at the new location. For example, you were looking at the visual placeholder or bad news location when delivering the bad news, so make more eye contact at the new location. If your voice was slow and monotone, change it to fast and variable. If your weight was on both feet, place your weight over one hip more than the other (a more casual posture).

In Chapter 2, How the Signals Work, we learned how to create trust, while in Chapter 3, Gestures of Relationship, we learned how to help the audience feel self-confident, capable, and good. Locations build upon those elements of rapport and add the concept of safety. People need to feel safe to have open and honest communication. By systematically selecting locations, you can avoid being seen as the bearer of bad news and dragging toxic situations around with you. It creates an effective atmosphere for your message to be received in the way you want it to be received. Using locations lets people know what to expect. Knowing what to expect helps them feel safe.

5 | Gestures
That Teach

People love to learn from other people. As with gestures of location, gestures that teach also use mime concepts. These nonverbal movement sequences tell a story or show step-by-step directions and are most often used to answer questions or problems of what, how, how much, and where. Gestures that teach are not about how perfect your representation is. They are about how comfortable most people are with visual learning. Attention goes where it is directed. The key to successful teaching gestures is the ability to keep listeners' eyes where you want them. If you are not looking at what you want them to look at, they will not be looking there either.

Gestures that teach simplify your message and make the speaker focus on specifics. Consistent and logical motions are an essential component of facilitating learning and memory by specifically directing the listener's eyes. There are two key skills with gestures that teach:

1. **You must look where you want the audience to look.** Listeners follow your eyes before they follow gestures. The listeners' eyes will follow your hand only if your eyes follow your hand. Directed listener eye contact must work in unison with the hand gestures. This is easily achieved by watching your own thumb as you make the gesture.

2. **There must be a logical reason for the gestures.** For example, in a step–by–step series of gestures to explain working with a box, each gesture looks like you are holding a box that has a consistent size and weight. If you add a knob to the box, the next gestures must take into account the knob and the box.

Keep the Gesture Simple and Familiar

When we use only words to teach, we make it necessary for our audience to pay very close attention to what we say. Using gestures when giving directions or teaching makes the audience less dependent on the verbal part of the presentation. The visual reminder created by gestures allows the listener two ways to remember: auditory and visual. It thereby increases the likelihood of accurate recall.

Gestures that teach can teach anything, even proper conduct. If you want the audience to raise their hands before asking questions, teach them nonverbally that raising their hands is the protocol. As you ask questions, raise your arm and slightly turn your hand back and forth while you ask a question, such as "Who is from out of town?"

One of the more common teaching gestures is holding a hand up and counting on the fingers. Many of us are familiar with this from childhood. I was recently attending a sold-out event where the young hostess got up on the table and shouted out instructions on how to get into the event. She offered four points: she held up her index finger and stated point one, and then dropped her arm to her thigh with a thud. She held up her index finger again and stated point two, and again dropped her arm to her thigh with a thud, and so on. It wasn't pretty from the nonverbal perspective. It would have been more effective had she held her arm in place and raised fingers to correspond with the verbal count. However, even without it looking graceful, it worked. The audience got it. Why? It was a gesture of teaching they were familiar with. Look for other cues and signals that already have the meaning you are seeking when you use gestures.

Consider another common scenario of presenting to a team. For example, it is your job to explain a step-by-step task with a box that your team is supposed to be able to perform.

At a Glance

"First, you take the box from the container, move it over to processing, and then add the knob."

What Your Mouth Says	What Your Body Does	The Message You Send
First, you take the . . .	Start on your right, grab two sides of the phantom box, flex your arms, and bounce up and down two inches to establish there is weight.	See the box? It is really here; it has weight.
box from the container, move it over to processing, . . .	Keep the same shape, slightly lift the gesture, and move left the same distance as the size of the phantom box. Lightly bounce the box. The light bounce reinforces the box has weight.	The box goes from here to processing; again, it has weight.
and then add the knob.	Keep the same shape of the box with your hands and move over to the left one more time, and lightly bounce. Move one hand to the top of the box to add the knob, and the other hand to the bottom to support the box. The audience will see all sides of the phantom box if you remain consistent.	This is how the knob is added. The box goes from here to delivery, and still has weight.

It takes a series of gestures moving in a logical pattern for the listener to see a sequential task. Sequences are expected to move left to right, based on the way we read in English. Most people gesture from their own left to right, which makes sense from their perspective, since it feels natural. However, it is not natural for the listener, as they see your series of gestures moving right to left. To demonstrate what you are saying, you want to use a sequential series of gestures beginning on your right and moving to your left. Why? If you are standing directly across from the listener(s), as is most often the case for a presenter, you're the mirror image of the listener. Communication for clarity is not what is easiest for the presenter, but what is quick and easy for the listener to comprehend.

In gestures of relationship, you learned to join two ideas by holding the gesture throughout the length of the pause. You can also use gestures to join phantom objects, such as the box and the knob, with the instruction manual. To continue our example, we left the team with a box and knob, one hand on the top of the box, the other hand at the bottom to support the box. "First, you take the box from the container, move it over to processing, and then add the knob. Once completed, it is delivered to shipping." Maintain the box shape of your hands and lift the box up and move it over to the left one more time, the same distance as before. Lightly bounce it up and down to show it has weight. Still holding the bottom of the phantom box in one hand, remove the hand holding the top of the box and gesture toward the location of shipping as you say "... where they will put it together with the instruction manual." Return your hand to the box as if your hand were clutching a manual. Place your hand holding the phantom manual on the side of the phantom box. Your hands will be one palm facing up holding the weight of the phantom box, the other palm sideways keeping the manual in place.

The best way to teach is to have your gestures model what you are saying. Gestures that teach work because the audience can follow along and believe you have a box with a knob and an instruction manual. Gestures that teach provide a foundation and frame the words with a series of visuals. This gives additional information that is not available with words alone. They force the listener to watch the speaker, and thereby elicit closer attention and a quieter environment.

Verbal and Nonverbal Congruency

Gestures that teach must be logical, used in a consistent manner, and congruent. Congruency occurs when your verbal and nonverbal match, a fundamental of all the skills in this book. To see congruency in action observe great communicators. Most often you will notice that the gestures and movements they make support the words they use.

Congruent messages are easy for the listener to comprehend quickly. An incongruent or muddled message has a far greater chance of creating misunderstanding. If the listener asks questions that you think you already answered or if they look perplexed with a tightened brow and a slight sideways tip of their head, then you've most likely sent an unclear message.

Congruency conveys that you expect attentiveness and are in control of yourself and the situation. To be an inspirational and influential leader you must portray self-control, and part of this portrayal includes the ability to send a cohesive, complete message, whether scripted or not. Sending such a message requires verbal and nonverbal agreement.

To send a credible, congruent message, use a voice pattern that is flat, not rhythmic. Maintain clear articulation as well as distinct pauses and controlled pacing of words. The nonverbals that are congruent or match the flat voice pattern are direct eye contact, limited blinking, use of a sideways palm or palm down gesture, and low breathing, plus erect posture and weight on both feet, toes pointed forward.

To send a friendly or connection-making congruent message, use a voice that is rhythmic and flows up and down while you lightly bob your head. Use palm up gestures with natural, casual eye contact. Posture can be casual and weight can be off-center when using the connection voice.

Do I Always Have to Be Congruent?

It's not mandatory to always have your nonverbals be completely congruent with what you are saying; it just makes things easier. In fact, you may not want them to match. My friend Sergio, true to his family culture, uses gestures that are larger and farther away from his body than someone from a Northern European culture. Sergio loves to tell stories. Each time you hear the story, it gets grander and grander with larger gestures. Sergio's gestures are congruent with his emotions and intent, since the purpose of his gestures is to support the scale of his story. Because his audience is so caught up in his dramatic storytelling, Sergio can get away with the randomness of his gestures—they add to the grandeur of it all.

Another reason you may not want nonverbals to match your words is to intentionally cause confusion. Mismatching the verbal and nonverbal can cause momentary confusion in the listener and is a common—although in my opinion, underhanded—sales technique. Causing momentary confusion in the listener makes them more open to suggestion.

Congruency allows you to relate to your listener, thereby building a relationship. It puts the mind at ease, and when the mind is at ease, it feels safe. Trust is a product of feeling safe and one of the cornerstones for establishing solid relationships. Congruence (match) versus incongruence (mismatch) is another technique for your toolbox.

Gestures that teach are a support system for our message. They create a simple pattern that is easy to follow and remember. "Let me show you" are four of the most helpful words someone can say, especially when used with teaching gestures.

6 | Gestures of Expectation and Influence

Gestures of expectation and influence reflect your day-to-day beliefs about your own and others' abilities. They show you are self-confident even when you are not, and they demonstrate that you have confidence in others. They are used to demonstrate beliefs, gain compliance, and influence behavior. In contrast, gestures of relationship, location, and teaching are short-term movements that support specific words or phrases. All the gestures are important skills, and over time they will become integrated into your baseline behaviors.

The behaviors we exhibit everyday are called baseline behaviors. Some, which are learned, we use because they've successfully achieved the outcomes we want. Others are innate behaviors. Incorporating the gestures of expectation and influence that display self-confidence, including relaxed arms; low, steady breathing; erect posture; weight evenly distributed on both feet, if standing; a voice that drops at the end of each phrase for business; and a rolling voice that goes up at the end for relationships, will pay large dividends in how others perceive you.

How to Use Your Posture to Show Your Confidence

You always want to display self-confidence, no matter how you are feeling inside. Don't let them see you sweat. If you are not confident, your audience or team most likely won't be confident either. So fake it until you make it by maintaining positive gestures of expectation and comfortable, low breathing.

Additional proactive nonverbal gestures of expectation and influence that display your self-confidence and expectation of competence in yourself and others include the following intentional body postures:

- Back straight to create erect posture.
- Shoulders square on spine and back, no slouching shoulders.
- Head squarely above shoulders and neck.
- Chin parallel to ground.
- Eyes open and focused on where you are going.
- Weight even on both legs, if standing.
- Gait steady and smooth, if walking.
- Breathing low and steady, with smooth abdominal movement.

Three positions of your forearms say "I am confident, we all know what we are doing, we are capable and I expect good things." Keep your forearms waist-high in front of your body, wrists at the same height as the elbows so that the forearms are parallel to the ground. Hands can be gently clasped (while it may be tempting to do, avoid twisting rings or picking at your nails).

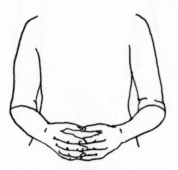

Keep both arms at your side, hanging straight down, which is a natural walking position for the arms.

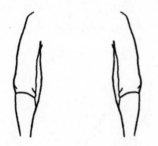

The combination is one arm at your side and the other forearm at your waist parallel to the ground. Think TV weatherperson pose or a queen carrying her handbag. This works well if you have something to hold (like a pen or notebook). However, be careful, it is easy to alter the meaning of this gesture. Avoid the gesture of self-reassurance in which one hand reaches across to touch or hold the other arm, most often at the elbow, or—a favorite of politicians—to adjust the sleeve or cuff link. While some think this works for politicians, it is a stalling, gather-my-thoughts self-reassurance gesture. To convey a high expectation, the parallel hand does not touch the other arm.

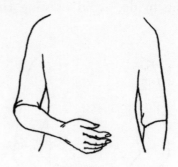

The five most common gestures that convey a lack of self-confidence are the fig-leaf hands, hands or thumbs in pockets, hands behind the back, arms crossed over the chest, and hands on hips.

Fig-leaf hands. Your hands cover the groin region and visually make you look smaller. Your body says, "I'm harmless" or "I'm afraid."

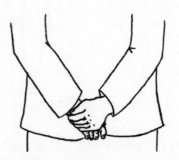

Hands or thumbs in pockets. Thumbs hanging off the pockets and hands deep in both pockets both say something similar to the fig-leaf hand gesture, "Geez, I hope you like me." Hands deep in the pockets jingling change say one of two things, depending on context, "Geez, I'm nervous and hope you like me" or "Geez, I'm so bored. Is this ever going to be over?"

Pockets and waistbands can convey multiple meanings depending on where the hands or thumbs are placed. Thumbs tucked in the waistband usually say, "I am staking my territory," which is a gesture of power, not influence. Thumbs displayed while the hands are tucked in the pockets say, "I know I am superior and I believe I have dominance." Pockets and waistbands are not a good place to rest your hands. They are not advised in business situations if you want your body to send a consistent message of confidence in self and others.

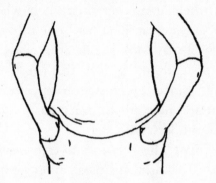

Hands behind the back. Hands grasped behind your back can be seen as either "Geez, I hope you like me" or "You better fear me," depending on context. Neither one is good, so avoid this position altogether. In the first scenario, a person looks smaller without covering the groin. Since people often do not know what to do with their hands, they will start with the fig leaf and quickly move their hands behind the back when they realize where their hands are. In *you better fear me* the hands behind the back are one behavior in a pattern:

- Hands grasping each other behind the back.
- Posture erect with weight squarely over body.
- Gait slow and steady, if walking.
- Head held high with chin parallel to the floor or slightly elevated.

This is what I like to call a royal strut. Your body utilizes this pattern to convey superiority, extreme self-confidence, and *I know I have power.* Subordinates often mimic this pattern when their manager isn't around, but would never dare to do it in front of the boss.

Arms crossed over the chest. This stance is most frequently understood to be discomfort, whether you are judging, upset, cold, or just have gas. In business, others may interpret it as "I am not open to discussion" or "I am annoyed." People habitually cross their arms over their chest when listening or waiting, so this gesture can be a hard one to overcome. Those who know us well may look at our arms across our chest and think nothing of it, thinking "Oh that's just what John does when he listens." Since the crossed-arms gesture is one of the most misinterpreted nonverbals, don't do it. Why give others the chance to misunderstand?

Hands on hips. This is a *ready-to-take-action* gesture, think gunfight at the OK Corral. It makes most people appear bigger, because they are actually taking up more space. If the arms across the chest doesn't sufficiently display the level of annoyance desired, the hands on hips can be the fallback position. There often is a gender difference to the hands-on-hips annoyance pattern:

- A male will have his weight centered and both feet firm and squarely under his hips, drop his chin, frown, and perhaps even pull up his pants before placing his hands on his hips.
- A female will stand with one leg slightly forward and her weight on the back hip. This allows her to tap her toe for extreme annoyance. She places one or both hands on her hips, drops her chin, frowns, and eyes go high in their sockets. She looks up and out as if over eyeglasses.

When it comes to inspiring and influencing others, we can say all the right words, but if our nonverbal postures send a different message, that is what others will understand and take away.

We often revert to our innate baseline behaviors when we're under stress, which compromises our ability to communicate effectively. When we are tense, our nonverbals can send confusing signals. That's when we are more likely to misunderstand other people and lapse into unhelpful patterns of behavior. It often helps to take a break to relax and breathe when managing our own baseline behaviors during stressful periods. It is a highly skilled leader who can maintain learned nonverbal baseline behaviors that reflect self-confidence, even under strained situations. Along with the body postures that display confidence, the silent, gestured pause from Chapter 2, How the Signals Work, and changing locations in silence from Chapter 4, Gestures of Location, are excellent tools to use to regroup on the fly.

Manage the Behavior—Not the Person

Once you know and are able to use nonverbal behaviors to reflect your high expectation of yourself, you can also influence a listener's behaviors. Over time, you begin to observe that if a behavior has appeared previously in a certain context, it could appear again if a similar context arises. Decide beforehand how to manage your own or another person's behavior should it reappear.

For example, Sally and Frank have worked together for years. Sally notices at the decision point of every meeting Frank is louder than the other attendees. While the other members appear shocked at his behavior, Sally knows that this is just Frank's style. When he gets excited, he goes above the other voices, waits for it to get quiet, and then makes his case. While this approach works for Frank, he would be more effective if he dropped to a whisper and leaned in. Sally isn't surprised and remains neutral by continuing to breathe low. She is used to Frank's behavior, but the rest of the group is not. Sally could choose to intervene with a gesture of *slow down* (both palms pressing down), or she could gesture to Frank to wait. She chooses to observe the group during this turning point of the meeting and make mental notes for next time. Anticipating Frank's behaviors has given Sally time to adapt her behaviors.

Side note: Sometimes, another person's behavior is best left alone. Observe nonverbal behaviors as a group or pattern, and do not read too much into a single nonverbal cue. Consider all of the nonverbal cues you or others are sending and receiving before choosing to respond. The ultimate goal is not only to know what your nonverbals are saying to others but also to know if you want your nonverbals to say anything at all. Often the difference between power and influence is not the technique employed, but the timing of that technique. Knowing when and if you should respond is a significant part of nonverbal influence. Once we understand when and if we want to use nonverbal cues and signals, we have two options: to be proactive or reactive.

Proactive versus Reactive

In the case of Sally and Frank, Sally was proactive in her response because she was used to Frank's habitual (baseline) behaviors. If she had not known Frank before the meeting, whatever she chose to do regarding Frank's behavior would be reactive. She still could have remained unresponsive. However, she most likely would have been shocked, much like the other members of the group. This might have led her to form an unfavorable opinion of Frank before they even began working together. Not understanding someone's behaviors in context often leads to judgments that later prove inaccurate. Business relationships and opportunities can be lost based on a reactive judgment.

This same concept applies to groups. If you know the behaviors that members of a group are likely to exhibit, you have a good understanding of how they will react in a situation. It is far better to proactively acknowledge a situation then to have to reactively repair relationships. Proactively acknowledging a possible disappointment, both verbally and nonverbally, diminishes any negative reaction to an expectation.

To proactively acknowledge disappointment open with the phrase, "I know some of you will be disappointed," to separate yourself from the group. Use "Some of us are disappointed," to be seen as part of the group. The corresponding gesture starts with your arms at your waist. Then extend your arms toward the audience at the same time you say "some of you" or "some of us." Depending on how the news is likely to be received, as you say "will be disappointed," choose a palm up gesture to say, "I'm one of you," a sideways palm gesture to say, "This is serious," or a palm down gesture to say, "This is just how it is."

Conversely, you can use gestures of expectation and influence to proactively empower diverse groups. Previously, you learned to join different objects or ideas. You can also nonverbally demonstrate an expectation for two diverse teams to join together to work on a common project.

Let's continue the scenario started in Chapter 2, How the Signals Work. The speaker said, "Due to the current dismal sales projections, the budget for this project will be X. You each bring so much talent to this project. This project will give all of us an opportunity to learn from the best." Now the scenario continues with the speaker nonverbally asking for cooperation.

At a Glance

"Members from production, please bring the timetable projections next week. And, engineering, please have the materials list available for accounting. So, everyone, let's work together and meet back here on Tuesday."

What Your Mouth Says	What Your Body Does	The Message You Send
Members from production, please bring the timetable projections next week.	With one arm extended from your waist, palm open and up, lightly bounce the gesture, and make eye contact toward the production team. Hold gesture.	I see production over there and am seeking cooperation.
And, engineering, please have the materials list available for accounting.	Extend the other arm, palm open and up, lightly bounce the gesture, and make eye contact with engineering; hold gesture. At this point, you have both arms gesturing to two places.	I see engineering over there and am seeking cooperation.

To nonverbally join the two groups, production and engineering, together:

What Your Mouth Says	What Your Body Does	The Message You Send
So, everyone, let's work together and meet back here on Tuesday."	Loosely clasp your hands together (keep air space between your palms), lightly bounce your hands up and down as you make eye contact with the entire audience and smile. Keeping hands clasped, extend your arms toward the audience as they leave. Hold gesture, and lower your gaze.	I am joining you together. We are now a team. We are still together, even after we leave today.

By moving both arms outward with open palms, you create a phantom location for production to be in one hand and engineering to be in the other. The movement of bringing the hands together in the gentle clasp relays the expectation of *joining* the two teams. You can place multiple items in each hand and join them together, as long as you remember what you place where and it makes sense to the audience. The bounce of the clasped hands and the smile reinforce that you are pleased with what is happening, thereby creating a nonverbal positive feeling of teamwork. By lowering your gaze you are dismissing the teams to go work on the project.

I Expect You to Wait

A friend and I were attending a workshop given by a young attorney who was offering top-notch information. Despite the fact that she was presenting relevant material, her skills at understanding what her body was saying to the group were limited. Unfortunately, this hampered her ability to manage an individual with bad behavior. She had a know-it-all in the room who kept peppering her with comments, such as "Yeah, but...," "What about...?" and "By the way...."

I'm sure you know the type. In this case, the know-it-all really destroyed the flow of information and sent the speaker into a tizzy. She was shifting her weight from leg to leg and her gestures were jerky. She politely stopped and answered each outburst. After a while, the group felt as though we were simply watching a personal conversation between the heckler and the attorney. The attorney's breathing became shallow and high in the chest, and her movements became stiffer, indicating she was getting distracted and having trouble concentrating. She didn't know what to do, so she called for a short break.

Luckily, my companion approached her and asked, "My friend is a presentation coach. If she could show you one or two techniques that would stop the heckling behavior, would that be of interest? We promise to take only one minute of your time." At that point, of course, she was happy to try anything.

Side note: Why did my companion ask the presenter on my behalf, instead of my offering help directly? She did so out of respect. It is easier to tell a third party, "No, thank you" than to refuse help from the person directly offering it. This is about respect for the other person's well-being. After all, the attorney may not have been open at that point to feedback or help. Part of being a good communicator is knowing when and if you can be of service. Sometimes people are not open to what you have to say or to your help and that is okay.

I offered the following advice: "First, try ignoring the heckler. Do not respond to the questions. If his behavior continues, verbally remind him of the scheduled Q&A time by saying, 'Please hold questions until our Q&A time' while gesturing to a spot over there near the wall as if it were a Q&A location. If he starts again after the gentle reminder, look to the opposite side of the audience (away from him). Then, without looking at him, acknowledge nonverbally that you heard him by doing the following:

1. Move your arm closest to the heckler straight down your side.
2. Slowly bend your arm at the elbow to move your forearm about 30 degrees up from your side.
3. With your palm facing down, slightly cock your wrist back to expose your fingertips.

"Hold that gesture as you continue what you were saying, and do not drop it until the behavior has stopped for a while. A refinement can be that as you continue with the presentation, keep your gaze on the rest of the audience. Do not make eye contact with the heckler. As you continue to look around the room in the normal course of the presentation, have your eyes (eyes only—do not move your head) go up and over his head, then back down to normal eye contact with the rest of the group."

You may wonder how the *wait sign* can be respectful of the other person—in this case, the heckler. The wait sign works in most cases, but not all. Sometimes you just can't save a person from their actions. If the heckler did stop, it would save him embarrassment in the eyes of the group. If he didn't stop, however, it would save **you,** the presenter, in the eyes of the group.

In this situation, saving someone was not as important since the group's time together was limited. If it had been a group in which the heckler needed to maintain relationships, helping the heckler understand he was damaging his relationship with the group would be part of leadership and influence. If the heckler had continued, the wait signal would have acknowledged to the group that the heckling behavior was not acceptable. At that point, it would be more important to tend to the well-being of the audience and yourself as presenter.

Power Gestures

The attorney could also have used the gesture popularized in pop culture as *talk to the hand*. However, it is wise to start with small nonverbal management of another's behavior and increase as needed. *Talk to the hand* is a definitive power gesture. In most Western cultures, it plainly states **stop**. Use it wisely and only when the situation truly calls for it.

Using a power gesture can ramp up emotions. Therefore, before you do so, consider the amount of influence and/or power you may need to gain compliance. If you choose to use power gestures, the slower the speed of the gesture and the greater the bend of the elbow, the less aggressive the gesture appears. To produce the talk-to-the-hand sign, move your arm closest to the heckler straight out from your shoulder, ending at a predetermined bend in the elbow. At the same time the arm is moving parallel to the ground, the wrist bends 90 degrees up exposing the open palm with fingertips extended. Hold that position only until the offender complies. The longer you hold it, the greater the chance of damaging not only your message but also your reputation. Consider the amount of power needed to stop the behavior immediately, and if it's worth the collateral damage.

Collateral damage can come in several forms: the emotional upset of other group members or the destruction of your reputation or relationships within the group. Often when a leader resorts to power, others interpret it as just as offensive as the bad behavior the leader was trying to fix. The other members of the group will have one of two responses, "Thank goodness, finally somebody did something!" or "Whoa, if the speaker did that to him, would she do it to me?"

Depending on the group's culture, a speaker can actually split herself off from the group and encourage them to protect the heckler from the speaker's aggressive gesture or action. The opposite can also be true. Another group might applaud the speaker for taking action to stop the annoying person. The attorney could have requested that the heckler leave. She may have even raised her status within the eyes of the rest of the group if she had made the request while breathing low. It's vital to know the most likely response and meaning of your gestures with the given group and context before you use gestures that assign negatives, or that can be seen as power gestures.

How to Confirm Others' Perception of the Experience

Train yourself to be aware of the interaction between the group as a whole, the individuals within the group, and yourself. For example, most people observe and understand the simple *wait* gesture of the hand. It is one with which most are familiar from childhood. The audience's relief that something is being done about that person overrides the incongruence of the wait gesture with the continuation of your presentation. Sometimes the audience just wants to see you acknowledge that someone is misbehaving. Even if the wait gesture hadn't worked with the heckler, it would have confirmed to the audience that you saw it the same way they did. It is important to validate the perception of acceptable behaviors in the group.

I had agreed to help a fellow trainer, Steve, as a coach for his workshop, so I spent most of the morning sitting back and observing his presentation. One attendee, named Shellie, was not behaving like someone who was voluntarily attending an expensive two-day workshop. I couldn't understand why she was there. Her verbal response to the majority of the workshop was "I'm not trying to be difficult, but...." She would do a pecking point with her index finger (think of a chicken's beak pecking) at individuals she disagreed with. If she didn't like what was being said and her pointing wasn't strong enough (by her guidelines), she would let out a rush of breath and loudly move her chair and slouch back. Once she was dramatic enough to leave the room with two loud exhales trailing behind her. Shellie could have easily been labeled a nonverbal bully.

However, she thought her behavior was entirely appropriate. Her behaviors told me she was very self-selective and she was deciding her own reality. It is especially difficult to work with someone who already has all the answers. So what was Steve to do?

The short answer is nothing. Unless he wanted to resort to power, there wasn't much he could do. His only answer was to change how the rest of the group behaved. Since he had to maintain a working relationship with Shellie, telling her to leave was not his first choice, and it doesn't help much to talk to a bully in private. They will argue that you are wrong and they know what's best for the group. Nothing that Steve chose to say or do at that moment would have transformed Shellie or helped her understand how her behavior was isolating her from the group. It was obvious from her previous outbursts that Steve wouldn't be able to manage her behavior quickly through nonverbal suggestions, such as the wait gesture. What we had to do was figure out how to get the rest of the group to ignore her. We carefully observed Shellie's behavioral patterns and noticed that she was most intense when it appeared someone was wasting her time. Therefore, the moment Steve anticipated Shellie was starting one of her outbursts, he distracted the group by nonverbally indicating they should pick up a pen and paper and, using a whisper, he asked the group to answer a question. The incongruence of the whisper, combined with the noise and movement of the group, taught them to ignore Shellie.

As you consider how you might manage another person's behavior, remember that your goal is to manage the behavior, not the person. We want to leave the person's self-esteem intact. First, answer the following about the situation:

- What am I trying to accomplish?
- What are the desired results?
- What conditions are likely to change?
- When and how are they likely to change?

In Steve and Shellie's case, the amount of power needed to stop the behavior immediately was not worth the collateral relationship damage to and with the other people present. The other people present had expectations about how the group should function and how each person should behave. They tolerated Shellie's behavior even though subtle nonverbals told us that they knew it was disruptive. This group would have been more offended by Steve had he chosen to use power than they were by Shellie's behavior.

Take time to consider all those affected by your communication. Sometimes it is not just the person right in front of you. It may also be other group members, or those within the offender's sphere of influence. A sphere of influence comprises all those people affiliated with them (including yourself) who are affected by your decision (for example, a spouse, child, boss, team members, or community). Ask yourself, "Is what I am communicating affecting their (or my own) wider sphere of influence?" Then, consider alternatives before taking action. Your style of interacting with your audience will have a lot to do with your success. The more you can relate to your audience's situation, the more likely you are to achieve your desired outcome. Always remember the following important points:

- Consider the beliefs and values of your audience.
- Consider how the audience prefers to receive the message.
- Can you meet the outcome of the message and still meet the needs and desires of the audience?

Steve's group valued morale over productivity. They expected Steve to behave in a way that would maintain the well-being of everyone present, even if it allowed for disruptive behavior. That was the way things were done for this group, it had become routine. (Routines are simply long-running expectations.)

Expectations are funny things, and managing them can be elusive. An expectation is the assumption that something—usually unstated—is reasonably certain to happen. Managing an expectation is a two-step process. First, maintain the postures and gestures that demonstrate self-confidence. Second, carefully observe the individuals and the group to determine their beliefs and needs. Knowing the audience's beliefs and needs beforehand helps you understand what drives their actions and decisions.

Never assume that you and the audience have the same understanding of the communication. For critical messages, you have to communicate your expectations both verbally and nonverbally. In the following chapters, we will examine how eye contact and voice also influence the listener. Take the time now to examine your self-confidence and your relationships. Every effort you invest in developing self-confidence and demonstrating that you have confidence in the capabilities of others will pay you back tenfold.

7 | The Eyes Have It

Eye contact is the easiest and most immediate nonverbal that people notice. It can be subtle or direct, and knowing how to mix the two is a major part of the art of building relationships. How much is too much or too little varies with the culture, gender, and context. Eye contact works best when both parties feel it is *just right*. Therefore, take your cues from the other person and match their preference for how much direct eye contact to use.

Direct eye contact can be a nonverbal signal of confidence, yet it is one of the most overrated and misunderstood of the nonverbal behaviors. It is also the most often misused nonverbal. Many books suggest that if you don't make constant direct eye contact with someone, you are untrustworthy. Nonsense! I have even heard one expert recommend *gluing your eyes* to the other person when you want to make a good impression. I'm all for looking at someone when in conversation, but too much (or too little) eye contact is not only disrespectful but downright creepy.

It is okay to break eye contact. This happens naturally all the time during conversations. In fact, it is easier to process what you are hearing when you break eye contact. Many times we look away for a moment to follow the speaker's hand gestures or a distraction. Over the course of normal, positive conversation, eye contact is a series of long glances instead of intense stares.

Where Do I Put My Eyes?

There really are only a couple of places we can put our eyes during a conversation. We can look at the other person or we can look away. We often move our eyes away when we think or withdraw emotionally for some reason; we may be upset or allowing the other person time to be upset. Looking down signals a need for a time-out or break in the action. You can observe this technique watching the TV news. They look down and then pop back up to disconnect the last story from the one that is to come.

The way in which a person makes eye contact provides clues about their intentions. Eye contact is powerful, but rarely can it be used alone to express a complete message. Adding other facial expressions or body movements creates a pattern that helps the listener understand the entire meaning. Make note of the head position as well as the amount of direct eye contact. A tilted head with direct eye contact can mean curiosity, intense interest, or you are not being understood. Direct eye contact with an upright head position can mean you are engaged, you are serious, or it can mean you are confrontational—remember context rules.

To use direct eye contact in a business situation, position your eyes between the listener's eyes or just a bit higher. Imagine a triangle with the base below the listener's eyes and the peak of the triangle at their mid-forehead. Keep your eyes in the middle of the triangle to maintain a professional contact.

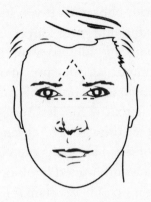

Eye contact has more latitude in personal relationships or situations. Here, you can invert the triangle so the peak is now at the other person's mouth. However, keep in mind that spending too much time in the lower half of the personal eye contact area (the inverted triangle) may be interpreted in a business setting as harassment or flirting.

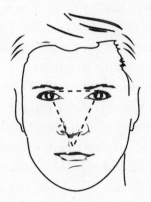

What Can I Do with My Eyes?

The rate at which you blink is also a form of giving or removing eye contact. We tend to blink more when we are under stress, so learn to control your blink rate. If you have a serious message to send, practice extending your direct eye contact without blinking. Limited blinking adds to your message's credibility. Actors use this technique all the time. For example, watch a close-up dramatic scene and count the number of blinks you see, and then compare that with a less serious scene. In a close-up, where we cannot see the actor's body language, the reason we feel the seriousness of the dialogue is the voice pattern coupled with direct eye contact and limited blinking.

Limited blinking is not a blank stare, often called the "deer-in-the-headlights" look or daydreaming. The blank stare indicates that the person is deep in thought and very associated with their emotions at that time. It is easy to spot. While they do have limited blinking, they are usually looking straight ahead or down. You can tell from the dilation of the pupils that they are not outwardly engaged. People in this condition have limited ability to listen and follow directions. Luckily, for most people, it usually does not last a long time or they can easily be snapped out of it.

When you open your eyes wide, your eyebrows and the corners of your mouth rise to produce the eye smile. While this is an engaging signal of approval, it's not always appropriate in business. Females use this more often than males. A subtler version is labeled "being coy." If you feel that you're not being taken seriously in the workplace, try to notice whether you are doing the eye smile and replace it with normal eye contact and a slow smile. This approach shows the signs of a discerning and confident person. If you are too quick to smile, others may wonder if it is genuine. The higher you are in the business hierarchy, the more flexibility you have with eye contact and whether or not to smile. A person who smiles very little is often perceived to be dominant and less friendly.

Eyes and Emotion

Eye contact is not the same as your eyes' response to emotional stimuli. Your eyes' response to emotions or outside stimuli, such as tearing up at a sad movie, cannot be easily manipulated, but eye contact can be. It takes little effort to shift your eyes away or lock your gaze.

Your emotional eye responses, such as tearing up, can elicit a similar reaction in another person. Research has shown that prolonged direct eye contact can actually increase another person's heart rate and speed of breathing. In extreme cases, acceleration in breathing and change in heart rate can leave a person hyperventilating or with a "fluttery" feeling, not unlike the feeling of falling in love. No coincidence, really, since one of the behaviors of the early stages of love is direct and prolonged eye contact.

Genders, cultures, and groups view eye contact differently. Direct and prolonged eye contact is more prevalent in Western cultures and is seen as a sign of respect when talking to a person in a superior position. In Eastern cultures, however, it can be a sign of disrespect to look directly at a superior. Although this is changing, make note to understand the different norms regarding eye contact when meeting people from other countries and cultures. Businesses also have cultures. Eye contact norms can vary with all types of cultures.

Women typically hold eye contact longer than men. The more intimate the conversation, the longer the direct eye contact. Men talking to men prefer less direct eye contact. As mentioned earlier, direct, prolonged eye contact elevates the heart rate. Between men the elevated heart rate can give a false sense of confrontation, aggression, or not being safe. If you have a hard time building rapport with a man, try standing side by side—both of you facing forward—looking and talking out into the foreground or down to the ground in an *aw-shucks, just-two-guys-kicking-dirt* position. This position can be effective when other attempts at rapport have failed.

The most important thing to remember is to always watch for cues from the other person or the group to understand when and how much eye contact is appropriate. Sometimes you just have to try eye contact to see how long it is comfortable for both parties. With a bit of practice it becomes natural. When the communication is friendly, and all signs are positive, eye contact comes and goes naturally.

Making comfortable eye contact while talking shows composure and conveys that you are paying attention, especially when you accompany it with a gentle nod. Look away from time to time, even if it's at the floor, to make communication seem more natural. Extended eye contact can mean there is either a strong interest or worry about safety. Since the same behavior can mean multiple things, we must rely on other factors to have a true understanding of how much eye contact is appropriate. The boss has much more latitude with extended eye contact, or lack thereof, than the employee. The higher an individual's status, the more latitude they have in breaking the social norms, especially facial expressions, including eye contact.

How to Manage with Eye Contact

The stereotype of management by eye contact is looking over the top of your glasses, as in the schoolteacher's stern look for talking in class. With or without glasses, the nonverbal message of the direct eye contact with the dropped chin, eyes high in the eye sockets is **stop**, you are being judged or watched. Managing others through eye contact can be more effective than a verbal reprimand; it can also help a person save face in a group. If you are in an authority position and this approach does not work, consider withholding eye contact, but only do so if you are in a position of authority. If you are in the lower position, you are sending out a message of pouting and pettiness.

Pros and Cons of Little or No Eye Contact

Little or no eye contact is often associated with lying, for example, "He wouldn't look me in the eyes." Untrained liars make eye contact about only 30 percent of the time during a conversation; therefore, "He wouldn't look me in the eyes" is true to a certain extent. Since the nonverbals of deception are easy to learn, it takes just a little practice for a professional or determined liar to maintain eye contact and breathe comfortably at the same time.

Lying is not the only reason people avoid eye contact. It might also be due to lack of self-esteem or interest. Sheila is an intelligent and articulate professional, yet many of her colleagues refuse to talk with her because of one particularly odd behavior. She speaks with her eyes closed, especially in one-to-one conversations. I will not speculate on why, since it doesn't really matter. The effect is simply that others perceive her to be lacking self-confidence and intelligence. If, like Sheila, you are shy and have a hard time holding eye contact, look at the listener's nose or forehead while you are speaking, or concentrate on their eye color. Closing your eyes is not an ideal alternative here, as it will only serve to increase the misunderstandings between you and the other person.

A reluctance to show emotions is another reason that some people avoid eye contact. In difficult or emotional conversations, use a visual placeholder—such as an agenda, form, or checklist—to have a place to put your eyes. Oftentimes when presented with emotional news, the last thing someone wants is to be stared at, as they feel the full weight of what was just said. The brain shuts down momentarily while it tries to sort out what it just heard. Having a visual placeholder gives you somewhere to put your eyes when you look away from the listener. Consider using both communication methods, verbal (auditory) and visual (placeholder), whether or not you are delivering difficult information.

Presenting information verbally without the use of a visual creates a sense of dependency on you—the speaker. The last thing you want as a messenger of bad news is to have the listener depend on you to repeat bad news. This just makes the bad news stick to you, since you are now the continued source. Having the information delivered two ways, both verbally and visually, allows the brain to process and remember the whole message.

Deborah, an office manager for a doctor, is in charge of handling the annual performance reviews for the staff. She developed a Performance Documentation Form, and throughout the year both she and the doctor keep notes on achievements and events. When Deborah delivers a performance review, she chooses a small table and sits at a 90-degree angle to the employee. Since she is right-handed, she sits to the employee's left so that her right hand is closest to him or her. Deborah would sit on the employee's right if she were left-handed. You want the hand you write with closest to the person. Another advantage of sitting at a 90-degree angle to the person is that it allows for easy eye contact by turning the head slightly to look directly at the other person or if she wishes to break eye contact, by looking at the form or straight ahead.

Deborah begins with a smile and some small talk. She makes eye contact as she acknowledges the employee's contributions and positive efforts. When it is time for the formal review, she refers to the Performance Documentation Form by using her right hand, palm up (closest to the employee) and gestures between the employee and the form. With this gesture of relationship (her palm up), Deborah is indicating the relationship between the employee and the form. Deborah's eyes follow her own hand as she looks at the form too. The pattern of looking and gesturing invites the employee to look where Deborah is looking.

As the employee looks at the form, Deborah does too. She does not look at the employee, which allows him or her to have an emotional reaction without Deborah watching. Deborah should use peripheral vision to monitor reactions and observe the employee's breathing, since an emotional reaction can momentarily stop a person's breathing. When hearing bad news, many people have a short, quick inhale and pull back their head in a startled manner. Once the employee has regained normal breathing, it is okay to resume appropriate eye contact to create the human-to-human connection again.

Sometimes people just don't want you to look at them, especially if you're discussing something emotional. It's respectful in difficult conversations to let someone save face by looking away. Most people start a conversation with direct, intense eye contact and—if the topic is emotional or intense—break eye contact on occasion to allow both of you to breathe. Of course, if the emotional stability of the listener or your safety is an issue, eye contact is necessary. If you don't have a visual placeholder to refer to, consider the thoughtful gaze by placing your hand on your chin and looking up, or the reflective gaze by looking down and nodding. Try a little experiment. The next time you are listening, break eye contact, look down, and nod. How does it make you feel? What was the other person's response? Note how you are both breathing. Did it become easier to hear? Did the speaker continue with the conversation?

Understanding how you convey messages with your eyes—as well as observing how other people use eye contact in both your professional and personal world—will set you miles ahead in your pursuit of communication mastery. Eye contact is one of the most powerful nonverbal tools we have. It can express hostility or love, callousness or compassion, regret or sympathy. Where you put your eyes and for how long expresses not only your thoughts but also your emotional comfort at that time. Here is another little experiment. Walk down a busy sidewalk and look at the people as you pass. Do they make eye contact in return? Who broke eye contact first? How long do you hold your gaze?

It is important to manage your eye contact, as it can easily give away what you are thinking and your emotional state. For example, if you see someone roll their eyes up and around quickly, you can be fairly certain they are disagreeing with whatever was just said. If they roll their eyes up and keep them there, they are just gathering their thoughts. Learn to monitor your own eye contact and movements along with those of other people. Eye contact often originates from our unconscious and can relay vast information as quick as the blink of an eye. Of all the nonverbal messages one can use, the eyes are the most expressive and really are the window to thoughts and emotions—if not the soul.

8 | How the Signals Sound— The Voice

There is an old saying, "It's not what you say, it's how you say it." Effective communication comprises infinite combinations of what we do with our gestures, body, location, voice, and breathing patterns. Now that you can easily recognize nonverbal patterns of gestures, let's look at the other nonverbal influences your body has and how they're intertwined.

With your voice, verbal communication is the words, and nonverbal is everything else. The common nonverbal components of voice include:

- Tone: warm, cool, bored, upbeat.
- Pitch: flat, low, high, ending up or down.

- Emphasis: too much, too little, where it is placed.
- Volume: too loud, too soft, just right, forced.
- Speed: pacing, tempo, cadence, rhythm.
- Culture: accent, pronunciations, slang, clichés.
- Emotion: happy, sad, afraid, excited, nervous.
- Facial expressions: smile, clenched jaw.
- Clarity: mumbling, stuttering, enunciation.
- Pause: make noise during, silent, length.
- Breathing: shallow, rapid, comfortable, forced, hesitant.

Of course, this is just a partial list of all the ways you can change your voice. Most people think that it's just the voice box or larynx where the vocal chords are located that produces the sound, but your vocal chords are only part of the sound-producing process. You can use this process to your advantage to change the emotional quality and perception of your voice.

The action starts in your brain, since your sound often mirrors your emotions. If you are feeling positive, your voice will naturally sound upbeat and energetic. The voice is a series of controlled vibrations. Where you place the vibration in your head (resonating chambers, such as in your nasal cavity or the back of your throat)—along with the way you open or move your mouth and tongue, and how deeply you breathe—all contribute to the quality of the sound you make. The more you practice control of airflow over the vocal chords and placement of sound vibrations as they travel through the resonating chambers of your head, the more control you have over how your voice sounds.

I met a resident physician the other day at my doctor's office, and my first impression was to doubt his competence. He had a habit of placing the vibrations in his nose and sinuses, giving his voice a weak, nasal sound. This is not the voice tone and resonance you would expect from a competent and confident professional. This is just one example of how the quality of your voice can lead others to make assumptions about your skill and expertise. Many voice nonverbals are habits and leftovers from childhood. Record your voice while reading a book or speech, and then listen for your nonverbal voice habits. You may be surprised at what you hear!

I will not go into great detail on sound and resonance. In short, each person has a unique vocal sound and resonance depending on the size and shape of their body, the influences of the cultures to which they belong, and their understanding of vocal techniques. Improving the sound of the voice entails opening the throat, releasing tension, and projecting the voice without straining. Experiment by making different mouth shapes and tongue placements while saying the alphabet to discover how each sound affects the resonance of your voice. Remember to do this with a full breath for the best quality sound.

Once you have mastered the nonverbals of the voice, including breathing, you have developed an integral nonverbal skill that is needed to build influence, trust, and safety. When it comes to tone, volume, speed, and other vocal nonverbals, different cultures have different understandings of what is normal. The most common nonverbal voice problems are:

- **Having a monotone voice.** Learn to vary the pitch by raising and lowering your voice to emphasize or deemphasize points. Culture plays a big part in whether someone naturally varies the pitch. When you're in a group, listen for what is normal for that group, and then adapt your voice to match. Believe it or not, they'll hear you better if you adapt your speed, volume, and tone to match theirs. You don't adopt their accent, just the cadence and pace. This is not mimicry, it's flexibility.

- **A forced or *announcer* manner of speaking.** There is a strained sound to this pattern, often caused by shallow breathing and running out of air. Nerves, tension in your throat and chest, even shortness of breath can cause the forced voice, or it may simply be a habit. The announcer voice has a fake cadence to it that sounds perpetually happy. To encourage the proper cadence, relax and imagine that you are having a conversation with a friend.

- **Being too loud or too soft.** Keep your volume consistent until you want to emphasize a point. A whisper can be as powerful as a loud voice. Know your intention as you change the volume. Consider the size of the audience and their location to determine the proper volume. Nobody wants to be yelled at and nobody wants to struggle to hear you. It is always good to check to make sure you can be heard, and if not, wear a microphone before you choose to shout.

- **Speaking too fast or too slowly.** Culture plays a big part in whether someone naturally varies their speaking speed. Watch for the baseline or normal speed of various cultures. If possible, try to match speed without looking fake. It doesn't have to be exact. If the listener is used to speaking and listening fast, they will have little patience for someone from a culture who speaks slower. It is sad, and not necessarily fair, but often fast talkers assume a slow talker has a lower intelligence. On the other hand, slow talkers often assume fast talkers are trying to put one over on them.

- **Nonverbals that don't match the words.** Your facial expressions can determine how your voice is heard. You can hear a smile, even over the telephone. If the voice pattern is flat and drops at the last word when you're asking for cooperation, people are doing so begrudgingly, because they heard something that sounded like an order. The reverse is true as well. If your voice has an up and down, almost a sing-song sound, and you're giving advice, most people will think your advice is not sound.

When you speak, other people read your voice just as they read gestures, therefore be aware of how you emphasize certain words. Simply changing the words you emphasize can change the meaning. For example, "I think the report is fine."

- Unconcerned: "I think **the report is fine**."
- Shocked: "**I think** the report is fine."
- Happy: "**I think** the report **is fine**."
- Worried: "**I think the report** is fine."

The nonverbals of the voice are so unique that you don't even have to be face-to-face to understand them. The best business voice consistently sounds clear, inviting, and under control. It helps if it sounds warm and upbeat too, but sometimes that is not possible. Bad news delivered in a warm and upbeat tone can leave the impression that you're happy about the bad news.

Voice Patterns of What We Do and Who We Are

You have already learned that when you use your nonverbal gestures in a random way, they may be out of harmony with what you are saying. You don't want to use your voice in a random way either. Your voice can also have intentional voice patterns and sounds. The voice patterns you use naturally are based on your family, friends, and the cultures of which you are a member (a baseline behavior). Voice patterns can also be associated with what you do (the job or position you hold), and where you are in the business hierarchy. The higher the position (CEO, owner, vice-president), or the more authority the position (police, military, school principal), the more options you have with intentional voice patterns in business. Business voice patterns fall into two main categories:

- **Credible.** People in higher positions within a business or positions of authority use this voice pattern most often.
- **Connection.** Traditionally, those in support or service positions use this voice pattern. This is also the voice pattern used to develop friendship or seek information.

How to Use the Credible Voice Pattern

The higher your position, the more permission you have to use the credible voice. This is the voice pattern to use when stressing or sending information and working with issues. This voice pattern maintains the same flat sound almost until the end of the phrase or sentence where it drops.

I have a long-time friend who recently retired from law enforcement. No one would argue that when you meet him, you realize he is one guy you don't mess with. He has what is commonly called command presence, part of which is the credible voice pattern. To create the credible voice pattern:

- Use clear articulation and pacing of words.
- Maintain a calm cadence.

- Maintain a flat sound until the end of the phrase or sentence, where the voice drops in sound with a chin drop. Drop the chin slightly as you end each sentence. The chin drop punctuates what you said with a period. The chin drop does two things: (1) it constricts the vocal chords, changing the sound and (2) it nonverbally reinforces what was just said.

- Use short pauses between sections of each sentence (where the comma would go), and longer pauses at the end of each statement (where the period would go).

- During each pause, breathe. Inhale completely filling the abdomen, keeping your head and lips perfectly still.

Your body should do the following to support the credible voice pattern:

- As you come to the part of the message you want to emphasize, maintain direct eye contact longer than normal. Limit blinking, but do not stare (staring elevates the listener's heart rate and can activate a fight-or-flight response).

- If the message is open to negotiation and you want to stress importance, use a sideways palm hand gesture. Tip your hand so that the thumb is up and the palm is to the side (neither up nor down). Note that women will often use the side hand gesture to mean they are not open to negotiation. The common understanding of the side palm hand gesture in business is that you are stressing importance or are on the fence about the issue. If you mean *not open to negotiation*, use a palm down gesture.

- If standing, have your weight on both feet and keep your posture erect. This is vital to being taken seriously. Keep your forearms at your sides or waist-high in front of your body, both of which convey confidence. Avoid the hands on the hips, crossed over the chest, or locked behind your back.

- If sitting, have your weight centered over your sit bones, and sit on the first one-third to two-thirds of the chair. Keep forearms away from the edge of the table or, if you must rest them, place the mid-forearm on the edge of the table. No elbows on the table, it is too casual for the credible voice pattern.

How to Use the Connection Voice Pattern

The connection voice pattern is used to seek information, soften news, and create an emotional connection. People in support and service positions often use the connection voice pattern. People who naturally use this voice pattern are often described as easy to get along with and helpful, and they develop rapport easily. To create the connection voice pattern:

- Use clear articulation and pacing of words. Maintain a rhythmic pattern that flows up and down and ends up, as if asking a question.

- End each statement with the voice going up—similar to a question mark. To accomplish this change of sound, move your chin up about 1 inch as you complete your sentence. This does two things: (1) it changes the length of the vocal chords, which raises the pitch and (2) it nonverbally reinforces that what was just said is about maintaining the relationship.

- Lightly bob your head as your voice flows up and down in a rhythmic pattern.

- Use short pauses between sections of each statement and longer pauses at the end of each statement.
- During the pause, breathe. The body and head can move.

Your body should do the following to support the connection voice pattern:

- Use gestures of relationship. For example, when speaking to another person, have your hand about waist-high, palm up, and gently move the palm toward the listener and back to you several times. This gesture indicates that the two of you have a relationship and seek information from one another.
- Make a connection with natural, casual eye contact. Keep in mind that looking away from time to time is normal.
- Mirror and match the listener's behaviors to establish rapport. This is not mimicry, but flexibility to create comfort in the listener. Avoid paraphrasing, as different words often have different meanings.
- If standing, you don't need to distribute your weight evenly on both feet. The connection voice pattern has more casual nonverbals, because it is primarily used to connect on the human-to-human level. It is used to build relationships and seek information, not to discuss business.
- If sitting, your back can touch the back of the chair or you can sit slightly off center.

You can use the connection voice pattern in the board room, but save it for building relationships, not formal business conversation. There is a high correlation between women and this voice pattern; however, it is not a female voice pattern.

Men who master the connection voice pattern are seen as more sincere and human.

Most people use both voice patterns naturally. Applying a systematic approach to your voice sends a masterful message. To refine both voice patterns and be seen as competent when using them, understand that the length of the pause in the credible and connection voice pattern is different. The credible voice's pause is longer than the connection pause. I visualize Morse code when I think of the pause and voice patterns. The credible voice pattern has slightly longer pauses than the connection voice pattern.

- Credible: statement (short pause) statement (longer pause)
- Connection: statement (really short pause) statement (short pause)

To be seen as both professional and personable, it is important to create a balance between the two patterns. It's part of communication congruency. The key with voice patterns, as with all nonverbals, is to know which to use and when.

Is Your Voice Sabotaging You?

As a nonprofit volunteer coordinator, Betty is a great recruiter for her agency. People like her immediately and find her to be incredibly helpful. She has no trouble getting people to show up to volunteer for events. However, commanding their attention when she assigns tasks is a real challenge.

Betty asked me why she can't seem to get people to listen, so I volunteered one Saturday to observe her in action. It quickly became apparent that verbally her voice was shrill and jerky, a voice nonverbal that others often assume is anger or distress. In this case, however, she was simply running out of air before she was able to deliver her entire message.

- Her breathing was high and shallow.
- She used verbal filler in her pauses, such as *aanndd* and *sooo*.

What her body said:

- Her weight was over one hip more than the other.
- She had one leg bent at the knee so that she could rock her foot on her tiptoe.
- She had a tight grip on the podium.
- When she gestured, which wasn't often enough, her arms were held tightly to her waist, and she quickly dropped the gesture.
- She used a seeking hand gesture combined with the connection voice pattern, conveying to the listener, "I'm open to discussion."

None of these behaviors expresses self-confidence and, grouped together as a pattern, they certainly don't say, "Follow me, I know what I'm doing." When I told her about the alterations that would help her get the message across more efficiently, she said it felt like a lot to change, and it was. Therefore, I advised her to simply practice one or two things each time she spoke. Three behavior changes that would most quickly improve Betty's ability to persuade others were:

- Changing her hand gesture to the palm down position when assigning tasks. The palm down says, "I'm **not** open to discussion." By consistently using the cupped palm up hand gesture (a beggar's palm) combined with the connection voice pattern, she was implying that she was open to negotiation.

- When assigning a task, use the credible voice pattern with the palm down gesture (to lessen the power implication, use a side palm gesture).

- Using the silent pause. Betty was addicted to the verbal pause. Her use of verbal filler in her pauses (such as *aanndd*, and *sooo*) made her sound less sure of what she was saying.

Addicted to the Verbal Pause

It is natural to pause when you speak—it's when you breathe. What's not natural is to fill the silent pause with *um, ah, uh, you know,* and other sounds. Verbal pauses are distracting and muddle what you are trying to say, because the audience sees you searching for the next words. Meaningless extra syllables or words make you look **less** intelligent. Your message will be more effective once you eliminate them. If you say a word and hang on it before you actually know what you're going to say next, it becomes a bridge word. The *um, ah, uh,* and *you-knows* are warning signs that you need to breathe. When you run out of oxygen and your brain starts feeding unintelligible words to your mouth, stop talking and start breathing.

EXERCISE: ARE YOU ADDICTED TO THE VERBAL PAUSE?

If you are, eliminating them is a two-step process of awareness and practice.

First, become aware of the verbal pause in others. Watch a nonscripted TV show, such as a news or talk show, and listen for verbal pauses. It may surprise you to find how many you hear. As you begin to notice the verbal pauses in others, notice if it changes how you feel about the speaker. Did you notice that they have a favorite verbal pause, for example, *you know*?

Second, the next time you have an important message to deliver, videotape yourself or enlist a friend to observe you and keep track of all the *um, ah, uh, you know, aanndddd, bbuutttt,* and *soooos*. Another way to monitor this is to replay a voice mail you left for someone. You'll find out very quickly if you are addicted to the verbal pause.

Working to eliminate the verbal pause may feel uncomfortable at first. However, the number of times you use it will decrease the more you practice. Practice often means saying a verbal pause and noticing that you did it. If you catch yourself doing it less often, then you are making progress. Eventually, the silent pause will replace the verbal pause. Remember, you don't have to fill every minute of airtime with noise.

The Need to Breathe

The cure for the verbal pause is to **breathe**. Breathing seems simple enough, so why would we bother covering it in a book about nonverbal communication? Because the most useful nonverbal I've learned is how to control my breathing. Breathing naturally and comfortably, no matter the situation, delivers a nonverbal message of confidence and poise; however, this is an often overlooked and underestimated nonverbal. Breathing is more than supplying oxygen to your lungs. It profoundly influences your mood, how your brain functions, how sensitive your nerves are, and how tired or alert you feel, as well as those around you.

So if it's so important, why isn't it in Chapter 1? Because breathing, while natural, isn't always easy to control. Just as your eyes respond automatically to emotional stimuli, so do changes in your breathing. Changing how you breathe in a situation is often reactive, not proactive. You can tell yourself to breathe low, full, complete breaths as you go face the board of directors, but the nervous system frequently takes over. Many times, you may not even be aware that your breathing has become rapid and shallow until you find yourself searching for words or feeling as though you can't think clearly.

There are two main breathing patterns that affect how others respond to us:

- Shallow, high, or rapid.
- Low, abdominal, or natural.

As with our ability to read others' nonverbals, we have an unconscious awareness of how others are breathing. It evolved in ancient times when we needed to be aware of other people's emotional states for our survival. When we observe someone else, we unconsciously make a mental note of how that person is breathing. The breath has four stages:

- The inhale
- Short pause
- The exhale
- Short pause

How fast you cycle through the four stages determines if you are breathing rapidly or naturally. When you're breathing rapidly, others often wonder if you are okay. This is perceived as a sign of distress, anger, fear, or surprise. It also keeps the fight–or–flight chemicals in a constant state of release. The human body constantly feels as though it is under some kind of threat. The fight-or-flight response is a genetically hardwired early warning system, designed to alert us to external threats. It not only warns us of real danger but also the mere perception of danger. Since breathing patterns are contagious, take care not to let yourself be affected by another person's high, shallow, or rapid breathing.

Shallow or rapid breathing is an asset when we need to release fight-or-flight survival chemicals for our safety, and avoid fully experiencing traumatic emotions all at one time. Research indicates that shallow or rapid breathing can keep us from fully experiencing emotions. Our breathing patterns and emotions are intertwined. Our emotions can cause us to breathe low and comfortably or shallow and rapidly. Conversely, our breathing pattern can change our emotional state. Do a little experiment. Quickly sniff (short rapid inhales through the nose) 10 times. What are you feeling right now? Most people feel a twinge of anxiety or anxiousness. That is the beginning of the fight-or-flight response. Monitor your breathing from time to time to make sure your breathing is sending a message of being confident and comfortable.

As discussed in Chapter 7, The Eyes Have It, eye contact also has a profound effect on how someone is breathing, as prolonged direct eye contact can cause a listener to go into shallow or rapid breathing. People under stress often start rapid breathing by holding their breath. Then, as they need to breathe, they constrict their chest muscles, which causes shallow breathing. When the lungs fill only partially, the body needs to get more oxygen. This increases the speed at which you breathe.

Those stuck in a rapid breathing pattern often sound afraid or angry, as the pitch and volume of the voice rise with the change of airflow. They are also at a loss for words and frequently use verbal fill-in sounds, such as *uhm* and *ahh*. If you receive comments such as "No need to be angry" or "Why are you upset?" it could be your rapid breathing that causes the misperception.

Consider the word *no* with a normal breath. The volume and sound is steady and even, and means something different than when it's delivered with a rapid burst of breath and at a higher volume and speed. The *no* spoken from rapid breathing has a more definitive sound that could be interpreted as angry. Some of the telltale nonverbals of rapid breathing and the resulting lack of oxygen—besides turning blue and passing out (which, of course, is a medical emergency!) are when:

- Movements appear jerky and stiff.
- The voice sounds differently, forced or shrill.
- Shoulders move up and down at a rapid pace.
- The head moves backward and forward at an exaggerated pace.

Low, abdominal breathing is the natural pattern in normal situations. The purpose of consciously breathing with long, slow, deep abdominal breaths is to bring the carbon dioxide and oxygen levels back in balance. It does not take too many rapid breaths to get your body's carbon dioxide and oxygen levels out of balance. Remind yourself to breathe with natural and comfortable breaths when confronted by stressful situations. The increase in oxygen will decrease your anxiety and soothe your nerves.

EXERCISE: PRACTICE YOUR BREATHING

Take a moment to observe how you are breathing right now. While sitting quietly, place one hand on your abdomen and the other on your upper chest, and count the number of cycles you breathe in and out per minute. An inhalation, pause, exhalation, and pause make one cycle. A normal inhalation and exhalation cycle is 12–14 times a minute when awake, and 6–8 times a minute while asleep.

Years ago I decided to take a belly-dancing class. I tried and tried, but I just couldn't get the swing of it. Finally, the instructor poked me in the belly and told me I was breathing backwards. I had no clue what she meant, and I never gave the comment a second thought until years later when a running coach mentioned that I breathed too high. What he meant was I had the habit of shallow breathing; and by bringing my chest up instead of out, I wasn't getting enough oxygen. I think unconsciously I taught myself to breathe by raising my shoulders because expanding out the tummy can make a girl look fat—so much for vanity! Keeping my body in a constant state of fight-or-flight wasn't good for me. Backward breathing can also be the result of wearing restrictive clothing or tight belts. Relearning to breathe naturally is a letting-go process. The more you experience the calming effect that low, abdominal breathing has on your body, brain, and voice, the easier it is to do in all situations. The goal is to maintain balanced breathing even while others around you do not.

Our breath supports all our nonverbals, most importantly, our voice. It is our breathing to which people react when they hear our voice patterns. How we breathe at the time determines if our credible voice pattern sounds definitive or angry, and if our connection voice pattern sounds friendly or pleading. When your audience is breathing low and comfortably, you are in rapport. If they are breathing shallow or rapidly, there has been a break in rapport, a distraction, or threat.

Remember the asset-liability scale: all behaviors including breathing and voice patterns are useful. Train yourself to breathe both shallow and low while using both voice patterns. You might as well expand your toolbox to contain them all.

9 | The Unintentional Nonverbals

So far, you've learned how to choreograph your gestures, eye contact, voice, and breathing to make an integrated message. Unintentional gestures are emotional reactions or the result of the body's desire for physical comfort and are often lovingly called *fidgets*. All can confuse the integrity of your message. An example of a physical comfort gesture is crossing your arms as you listen. In this example, the movement happens because of the desire for physical comfort, although an observer may assume you have closed yourself off. Movements made for physical comfort are just that. Remember, it is the pattern of behaviors and all movements that must be looked at in context.

Even though fidgets can calm us, those pesky, jerky movements or anxious behaviors often make others uneasy. Because they often become habits, they can be difficult to stop, so people usually try to disguise them. Adjusting a cuff link, rubbing an earlobe, and picking lint off clothes are just a few examples of the infamous fidget. While they're a comforting behavior, they send a clear, nonverbal signal of nervousness. Hands are not the only fidget offenders; there is a wide range of unintentional nonverbal fidgets:

- Touching the face and neck.
- Stroking or smoothing the hair.
- Rocking, swaying, or pacing.
- Vibrating your leg while seated.
- Clicking your pen or picking fingernails.
- Playing with jewelry.
- Inhaling, then blowing the exhale through the mouth.
- Laughing and sniffing.

The fidget list is pretty long, and gender does play a role in preferred fidgets. Women usually play with necklaces and twist their hair, while men rub their necks and spin their rings. It doesn't really matter what you do. Usually you're not even aware that you're fidgeting until someone points it out to you. Sometimes enlisting a friend to remind you is beneficial.

We fidget because we are nervous or anxious and this causes our breathing to become rapid. Rapid breathing and the resulting lack of oxygen often accelerate fidgety and anxious behavior and so a repeating cycle begins. In an oversimplified definition, nervous, fidgety, and anxious nonverbals are an automatic response from our limbic system. The brain's limbic system is hardwired to ensure survival and is, therefore, responsible for the fight-or-flight response. As we have evolved, this habit has taken on a different meaning. Rarely is our life in real danger, as it was when this response developed eons ago—our limbic system doesn't know this. Since you cognitively understand it, you can adjust your breathing and change fidget habits.

Fidget Reboot Button

The quickest way to calm yourself without a fidget or two is by pushing your own internal fidget reboot button: your breathing. Since you're nervous—and fidgety or anxious and nonverbal behaviors are so automatic—it can take a bit more effort to be aware you are doing them. If you know you will be entering a fidget situation, make an effort to become consciously aware of, and control, your breathing. Once you are aware, breathe with low, full abdominal breaths. The purpose is to bring the carbon dioxide and oxygen levels back in balance. Remember to maintain low, slow abdominal breathing.

EXERCISE: PRACTICE PUSHING YOUR FIDGET REBOOT BUTTON

1. Center your weight. If you are standing, have your weight on both feet. If you are sitting, balance your weight on the center of your sit bones. To center your weight, feel your strength and most of your weight in the space between your navel and groin.
2. Look straight ahead with your chin level to the ground. Have your throat as open as possible.
3. Take a slow, easy, deep breath and gently hold it. You should feel and see your abdomen (below the rib cage) expand.
4. Gently exhale through your nose until you see and feel the abdomen deflate.

5. Pause, your body will gently tell you when it is time to breathe again.

6. Repeat until you feel calmness settle over you.

7. Go through several slow, low, and steady breaths. You will begin to notice clear thinking returns as the carbon dioxide and oxygen levels get back in balance.

The biggest mistake I see when someone is learning to use the fidget reboot button is they are trying too hard. This is all about ease and flow.

Bringing more oxygen into your system calms and grounds you. Physical exercise also helps metabolize the excessive fidgets and oxygenate the brain—restoring your body and mind to a calmer, more relaxed state. If need be, take a break and go for a brisk walk. Your brain and breathing will thank you for it.

The Nonverbal Outburst

The nonverbal outburst is one of the hardest to hide and easiest to read. A fidget is simply your body's reaction to the need to be physically comfortable. A fidget comes from nervousness or anxiety. The nonverbal outburst or emotional gesture is a reaction that appears because your emotions are constantly expressing your likes and dislikes, satisfaction or dissatisfaction, warmth or disdain, and all your feelings on the subject and the person. They can also be related to other stressors, for example, the pressures of time. Say you meet a coworker in the hall and he decides to hold an impromptu meeting with you right there. You are late for a scheduled meeting, so you glance at your watch. He takes offense and lectures you that what he has to say is important. Your glancing at your watch was not related to what he was saying; it simply had to do with the pressure you felt about getting to your meeting on time.

Most movements and gestures are unintentional on the conscious level. They are an unconscious expression of how you are feeling at that moment. If you watch CSPAN, you can easily see unintentional gestures. Observe the gallery, not the speaker, and notice the nods of agreement or the back and forth head shakes of disagreement. These unconscious gestures let others know our emotions and thoughts at that time. The first step to conquering these movements is to know your emotions and intent *before* you start communicating—including listening, since listening is where the majority of the unintentional gestures happen that can short-circuit a relationship. It can be as overt as glancing at your watch or as subtle as a quick exhale. To be successful in communicating a clear message, you need to tune in to your own body language—especially the unintended nonverbals.

One way to control unintentional gestures is to use the nonverbal behaviors that display confidence, outlined in Chapter 6, Gestures of Expectation and Influence. When you are using the posture of self confidence, you are more aware of what your body is doing and less likely to use unintentional gestures. Play a little game with yourself. Walk around reminding yourself to breathe comfortably in all situations and use the self-confident posture for one week. Take note of how others treat you and how it makes you feel. The self-confident posture is:

- Shoulders square on spine and back, no slouching.
- Head squarely above shoulders and neck.
- Eyes open and focused on where you are going.
- Arms in the self-confident positions of by your sides or parallel to the ground or the combination.
- Low, steady, smooth abdominal breathing.

Slow yourself down before you have that significant conversation, and use the fidget reboot button before you walk into an important meeting. Display the nonverbal behaviors of confidence, and breathe comfortably so that your brain has all the oxygen it needs to support your voice and make you look and sound intelligent. The results may surprise you. You may find that people are more agreeable, and that you're able to accomplish more. Breathing low and fully not only stops fidgets cold, it makes you sound intelligent and revitalizes your emotions, thinking, and body. What person wouldn't want a simple and powerful tool like the fidget reboot button in their set of persuasive communication skills?

Now that you are displaying the posture of self-confidence, what behaviors can you use to display your confidence in others? It could be as simple as a smile, more eye contact, or maybe an appreciative palm up gesture or nod. Try a few and see what happens.

10 | The Fine Print in Your *Owner's Manual*

Throughout the book, I've mentioned that we all have an *Owner's Manual* that is wide open to all who know how to read it—and this chapter is going to prove it to you.

We know that we would rather do business with those we like and trust. Nevertheless, why do we get along better with some people, and struggle to build relationships with others? It's just part of our *Owner's Manual*. People are not all the same and one person isn't consistent all the time. Your behaviors change depending on how you feel, the context of the event, and others' feedback. However, there are certain baseline behaviors you tend to favor.

The Trick Is to Remain Flexible

Forming quality relationships with various types of people requires an understanding of how and why we are alike and different. We all use words to describe our thoughts; those words tell others more about us than just our education level. There are also corresponding nonverbals that go along with the words we choose. Together, these two elements tell others about our internal world, or our mind's eye. The nouns and action verbs we choose often describe how we internally represent our reality.

If you remember with pictures and see your thoughts, then you probably tend to use more visual nouns and action verbs to describe what you are thinking. If your memories and thoughts are based on sounds—and are more auditory in nature—then you likely tend to use nouns and action verbs that reflect the sound of your thinking. The words you use reveal your thinking processes and how you store your memories.

Our sensory preferences leave clues, both verbally and nonverbally. The literature, based on neurolinguistic programming's representational preferences, defines three different sensory modalities we use to learn, store (memory), and communicate via our primary senses: visual [V], auditory [A], and kinesthetic/tactile [K]. While smell and taste are also sensory factors, people who favor one of these modalities to represent their internal world make up a very small percentage of the population. The research also defines how knowledge of these modes of operation can be applied in everyday life. Recent studies have added a system called auditory digital [AD]. This is the only one of the representational preferences not related to our senses. Auditory digital processing is the language and actual words that we use and how we abstract the information from our senses and put it into language. It seems to be a second layer for one or more of the other sensory representational systems. This system is different from auditory processing, even though both involve sound. Auditory preferences are for the actual sound. Instead of saying something "sounds" a certain way, a person with a preference for AD may say, "That's logical" or "That makes sense." Auditory digital involves the meanings behind the words and symbols and it's something that I have long suspected is a consequence of modern life.

People are rarely only one of the modalities. Don't limit yourself by believing that you're only a visual person. Everyone uses all the learning modalities, but generally there is one that is more dominant or that you tend to favor. Of course, sensory modalities are only part of the story. Gender, culture, and context play roles in the choice of a person's sensory preferences. However, by listening carefully to someone describe their world—especially the action words they use—and noticing their behaviors, you can understand how they are viewing their reality. One caveat: By watching behaviors and listening to word choices, you can't tell what a person is thinking. You can, however, learn **how** they are thinking and which system—V, A, K, or AD—they're using at that time.

Action words are occasionally easier to elicit if you ask a question. If, for example, I asked you to describe a picture, you would most likely use visual predicates. However, if the question itself left you with a choice, you would tend to use action words from the representational system you prefer to share your mind's eye with the outer world. Examples of representational action words are:

- **Visual action words:** "I see it like it was yesterday" or "I get the picture."
- **Auditory action words:** "That doesn't sound right to me" or "That rings a bell."

- **Kinesthetic action words:** "I'm rolling with it" or "I follow my gut."
- **Auditory digital:** "That's logical, I can proceed" or "That makes sense."

The other two representational systems are less common:

- **Olfactory:** "There's a distinct smell in the air."
- **Gustatory:** "It's a taste of things to come."

The likelihood of being heard and understood is greater if both the speaker and listener are using the same representational system. For example, if you are speaking with a person who prefers the kinesthetic/tactile system, you would do best to express your thoughts and ideas with action verbs, such as felt, grasp, handle, and connect—along with the corresponding nonverbal characteristics, such as standing close as you talk, giving a pat on the back, or sitting casually in a chair.

Master the Behavior Game

Visual Qualities—People With This Inclination Tend To

- Stand or sit with head and/or body erect and with eyes wide open and alert, almost as if they're taking snapshots to remember what is happening.
- Memorize by seeing pictures.
- Be easily distracted by movement, since it shakes up their pictures.

- Look where they are going first and lead with their eyes when moving. They rarely bump into things, since they usually see them coming.

- Be high-chest breathers, who breathe from the top of their lungs with short, quick breaths.

- Sit forward in the first one- to two-thirds of the chair, with their backs rarely resting on the seat back.

- Be organized, neat, and visually put together. They know what goes with what when they dress.

- Be interested in how other people look as well, since appearances are important to them.

- Have a large personal space/comfort zone. They need room to see and make their pictures, so give them space when you can.

- Sit in the back of the room to see the entire landscape.

- Have trouble remembering verbal instructions, because their minds tend to wander to find visuals. (Always use written materials to back up verbal instructions with people who have the visual preference.)

If you picture yourself to be someone with visual preferences, you can probably see, from the above descriptions, why and how friends might call you judgmental, stiff, or a goody-goody. Just tell your friends you have such great posture because you have to hold yourself still to make the pictures you need to understand the world. If you want to change the impression you're sending others, take several deep breaths to fill your abdomen (which is good for your health, too); relax a bit when you sit and stand; use the backrest of a chair on occasion; slouch every once in a while; or really shock your friends and wear a rumpled shirt sometime. If you want to acknowledge someone with visual qualities, remember they like certificates, awards and visible displays of excellence.

Auditory Qualities—People Who Prefer This Approach Tend To

- Move their eyes side to side (ear to ear) while talking and thinking.

- Have to complete a story once they start it. If the story is interrupted, they will start over at the beginning, or at least recap the beginning of the story.

- Show an interest in what you have to say—as long as they can share their story too.

- Have moderate need for personal space/comfort zone. They will stand within earshot.

- Be easily distracted by noise.

- Talk aloud to think. They may have been trained not to have sound come out, but they move their lips when they talk to themselves—they hear their voice internally.

- Repeat things back to you easily and learn by listening. They enjoy talking on the phone.

- Be able to hear a song once and sing it note for note. They are often good at sound effects and other languages.

- Hear and memorize steps, procedures, and sequences to an internal rhythm.

- Have difficulty being silent, and do not know when not to talk.

- Hum, click their tongue, or make other noises. When asked to be quiet, they will swear to you (with a straight face) they were being silent.

- Quickly get on the nerves of a group by asking many questions and giving too many directions or examples.

- Be the life of the party, as they often tell a great story.

If the description of the auditory preferences rings a bell, you might have heard the labels "Chatty Cathy" or "needy," and been told that you never listen. People with the auditory preference can have a hard time getting along with others, especially those with visual preferences, as the auditory person's *noise* can upset a visual's *pictures.* People with visual preferences may consider those with auditory preferences annoying. Auditory inclinations can be a bit harder to change and adapt than visual or kinesthetic tendencies, but it can be done. It will take conscious effort, however, to become comfortable with silence.

My friend, Amanda, used to bribe her young son by challenging him to stay quiet for 30 seconds, then 1 minute, then 2, and so on. He still displays an auditory preference as an adult, but understands how the constant noise can disturb other people. If you have an auditory child, it is a great gift to help them learn to be comfortable with silence when needed.

If you want to acknowledge someone with auditory qualities, remember they like to be told how they're doing and respond to the sound of the voice or words of praise and compliments.

Kinesthetic Qualities—People Who Are Tactile Are Inclined To

- Breathe deeply, moving the diaphragm and filling the lungs to the point where their lower abdomen physically moves in and out.

- Move and walk slower than people who prefer other representational systems.

- Lead with their feet and tend to bump into things, as they move first then look.

- Have a close physical comfort zone. They will stand closer to a listener than a person with the visual or auditory preferences.

- Need to move their body, or memorize by movement, doing or going through the motion. They also use muscle memory, and respond when asked about a memory, "I feel like it was yesterday" or my favorite—something that really tells me they have a strong kinesthetic representational preference—"I pulled it out of my butt."

- Slouch, spread out, and appear very comfortable even when seated in important meetings.

- Have a rumpled appearance. They may not notice that their shirt is wrinkled or that a button is missing.

- Operate in an environment that appears disorganized, yet know the exact location of each piece of paper in their filing piles. They have a strong ability to keep track of where their things are.

- Show interest in what you are saying or doing when it feels right. (As with visuals, though, you always use written materials to back up verbal instructions, to give them something they can grasp.)

If you feel that the description of the kinesthetic preferences pushed a button, you might have heard the labels fidgety or messy or been told that you never sit still. In short, movement helps you think. You love to get comfortable and may slouch in a chair or throw a leg up over the arm. While a person with a kinesthetic preference is different from hyperactive, it is a challenge for them to sit still, since they truly learn by doing. School can be difficult for kinesthetic people; it has nothing to do with intelligence, just their preference for the kind of environment in which they learn best. Schools, especially those in the United States, are more geared toward visual learners.

The ability to take in cognitive information by touching and doing is slower. Representing things in memory through the visual or auditory senses has an advantage, since both visual and auditory information is available all at once, making the input into memory and output into speech quicker. However, the gut response or intuition of a kinesthetic is faster, and their think-versus-react response time is quicker. Give a person with a kinesthetic preference something to do with their hands or body, and they'll complete it extremely rapidly. These are the people you want available to respond in emergencies.

If you want to acknowledge someone with kinesthetic qualities, they respond to physical rewards like a pat on the back or high-five. They like to touch things and people. (Let's not get into any legal discussions about this preference; they just prefer to use this sense above others.)

If these descriptions feel all too familiar to you, then you prefer the kinesthetic system. If you wish to change the kinesthetic nonverbal message, the quickest way is to adopt some of the visual system behaviors. This can include sitting on the first one-third of the chair from time to time, remaining still while you talk, using smaller gestures, and walking upright with good posture.

Auditory Digital Qualities—This Group Prefers To

- Learn by working things out in their mind first.
- Be attracted to work that involves analysis, planning, and organizing.
- Have a need for order and to make sense of the world, to figure things out.

- Debate with themselves (head will tilt slightly one way and then the other, for the two sides of the debate) and carry on conversations in their head.

- Swear they discussed something with you when the actual conversation never occurred. It took place only in their mind.

- Dislike surprises and need to think something through and write things down.

- Need facts, figures, and logic to play a key role in the decision-making process. However, this does not necessarily mean they think in sequential, step-by-step methods.

- Be good at categorizing and summarizing and have a strong need to make sense of things.

- Use others as a sounding board for their ideas.

- Be critical of self and others.

- Use words and phrases that don't indicate any specific representational system, such as "this makes sense," "is logical," "has a reason," and "meets criteria."

If the auditory digital makes sense to you—and you have been labeled an absent-minded professor by coworkers—then most of these tendencies will correspond with you. Not everything needs to be logical. Sometimes it can just be because it's fun. If you wish to change the message you're sending, get out of your head occasionally and work to strengthen your secondary system or even incorporate some aspects of all the other systems. If you want to acknowledge someone with auditory digital qualities, they respond to sincere compliments that are specific and relate to the work performed.

While we all have a preferred representational system, we can easily switch, use, and adapt other systems depending on context to help build rapport. Avoid labeling yourself or others as a strict Visual, Auditory, Kinesthetic, or Auditory Digital. It is far more important to understand the qualities of each system and respond accordingly to master your message.

Remember, we are most comfortable with people like us. This doesn't mean that we're faking it. It simply means that we have positive intentions to adapt to other people's ways of seeing, hearing, and experiencing their world. If those with whom you are interacting are using patterns that indicate a visual preference, choose visual words so they can quickly *see* what you are talking about. For example, "The way I view it. . . ." Choose movements and actions that put them at ease. Allow a larger personal space than you might normally prefer so they can see what's happening.

If the person with whom you are interacting uses patterns that indicate an auditory preference, choose auditory words. For example, "That doesn't sound right to me" or "I hear you loud and clear." Choose movements and actions that put them at ease, such as allowing them to tell the story or provide background information. Use words of praise more often than you normally do.

There is no singularly *perfect* set of nonverbal and verbal behaviors and traits that will make you a flawlessly influential leader. Indeed, it is the flexible leader—the one who is accustomed to a wide variety of behaviors and knows when to use each—who is the most influential. In addition, flexible doesn't mean just using behaviors that will elicit a response. It also requires that we be willing to meet others on common ground, in this case, adopting common nonverbal behaviors.

11 | Putting It All to Work

The best communicators have learned to choreograph their body language to what their mouth is saying. As you begin to use intentional gestures yourself, the timing might feel slightly off. This can be because of the way your brain works. Usually, your brain is sending gestures to your body at the same time you are formulating your words. When you are first learning how to use intentional gestures, you formulate the words, and then match the gesture. This causes a slight break in the smooth rhythm and flow found in unconscious gestures.

The art behind the choreography is in understanding the intent and the underlying emotions of the communication beforehand. You should be aware of your intent before you begin speaking. Figure out how you feel about the message and why you feel that way. The three questions to answer before you begin to speak are:

1. What emotional message am I trying to convey?
2. Am I sending or seeking information?

137

3. How do I continue to build a relationship with this message?

Once you have these answers, rehearse your communication and notice if the feelings your message evokes are the same as your answers. If not, your audience will notice. Your intentions are a driving force behind the probability that others will believe your messages. You can't fake intent. It will show no matter how hard you try to mask it. Even if one is skilled at deception, others still intuitively notice their intent. People will get a feeling that something just isn't right.

Feelings Change Facts

Emotions—not just your own, but the listeners' as well—play the primary role in how your communication will be received. It is easy for you to understand what you want to communicate. You use your logic to do that. However, it is surprising how few people can as easily understand the emotions behind their communication. Ask yourself the following:

- What is my current emotional state around this message?
- What will most likely be the listener's emotional state upon hearing the message?
- Do I have the ability to manage my emotions appropriately?

Once you understand how you are feeling right now, it is important to answer the following:

- How might others feel upon hearing my message?
- What if the listener cannot manage his or her emotions appropriately?

People rarely change or make choices based solely on facts and figures. Decision making is most often an emotional process, followed by rationalizing the decision. Getting results, action, or buy-in depends on getting an emotional commitment. For the listener to commit, he or she must be able to:

- Understand the context, issue, or problem.
- Feel a sense of urgency to join you in solving the problem.
- Have the skills or access to skills to solve the problem.
- Feel emotionally compelled to act.

Understanding how someone else might feel builds safety, trust, and respect, all of which are cornerstones for rapport and lasting relationships. Inspirational and influential leaders gain support for their message by conveying simple, transparent, and heartfelt messages that address the situation, the solution, and people's emotions. They remove barriers to two-way communication by being open to feedback and creating multiple ways to communicate, such as in-person, e-mail, videoconference, and telephone.

Emotions Motivate

You can create a simple, transparent, and heartfelt message to answer both your own and the listener's issues and needs. You want the listener to understand the logical reasons and feel an urgency to move, and you want to support him or her by making sure he or she has the necessary skills needed to generate success. However, remember, it is the emotions that motivate.

The goal is to know your intent and underlying emotions before you speak, then hone your perception and intentional gesture skills to the point where you observe, understand, and react to behaviors without having to think about it. You quickly adapt to interacting in a style that is best for the listener. As I've pointed out before, this is not manipulation, this is flexibility. The point is to meet people where they are, and this requires that you answer the question: How flexible am I on my desired outcome? Truly inspirational and influential leaders consider the best interests of everyone involved. Short-term manipulation defeats the purpose and results in damaged relationships, destroyed trust, and loss of credibility and is not worth any momentary gain. It's like the sign that my assistant posted in the office after a particularly rough week: "Blessed are the flexible, for they will not be bent out of shape."

How to Communicate a Clear Direction

Whether you're trying to join team members with the expectation that they will play nice together, saving a heckler from his own behavior, getting buy-in on key initiatives, delivering bad news, managing top talent, or igniting passion for people to believe, the process of motivating change—especially with an uncertain outcome—occurs one conversation at a time.

You have seen how attention goes where it is directed with intentional gestures. Emotional attention goes where it is directed as well. Therefore, you must actively work toward the good and upbeat points in your messages and relationships. When you must speak of negatives, such as pointing out that profits are way down, remember negative away from and positive toward you! Consider your positive intentions, the corresponding emotions, and the desired outcome first as you begin to use these techniques. One way to teach yourself to understand the power and interplay of emotion and intent is to observe other people.

Observe to Become Self-Aware

On the surface, your message seems clear and your mouth and body say the same thing. However, you can never be 100 percent sure how others are interpreting you. You can only control your part of the message. Observe other people's nonverbals as they talk with you, while consciously taking note of how the interaction makes you feel. Replay in your mind, *What would I have done differently, if anything, to have a better interaction?*

Careful observation gives clues to what was successful and what was not successful. I always ask myself, *What did I see, hear, and feel that led me to believe . . . ?* The answer can be a powerful game changer. It places you outside yourself in the role of an interested bystander, watching the communication as if you had no stake in its outcome. Knowing why something isn't working is more helpful than knowing it worked. It is this analysis that trains you to make decisions about which intentional gestures to use next time.

So practice these skills. Start with one a week and make a mental note about what you saw, heard, and felt each time you used an intentional gesture. Try to observe the listener's response from their point of view and from the role of interested bystander. Watch for small as well as big changes. Sometimes cues are subtle. Did you observe the listener's faint smile when you offered a gesture of relationship as you talked about good news?

How Context Controls the Message

Because people are so adaptable, it is usually less accurate to evaluate small snippets of body behavior without knowing how someone usually behaves (baseline behaviors), the context of the situation, or his or her current emotional state. We all act differently in different situations. We are one way around our siblings and another way around our coworkers; therefore, blanket statements about behaviors are not recommended. No one is *always* or *never* one way. By adjusting a few nonverbals, you can change how others respond to you, and if you can alter your behaviors, so can others.

Remember, observing behavior is different from labeling it. Stay away from the temptation to label behaviors as good or bad. Note the difference between the two:

- She walked with her head tipped slightly up (observation) versus she is stuck-up (label).

- His weight is on both feet, his arms flexed, his chin is parallel to the ground (observation) versus he's ready for a fight or he's stubborn (label).

You want to become skilled at observing others so that you can adapt your message in real time. The quickest way to understand the messages and feelings you elicit in others with an intentional nonverbal is to observe the reactions you get in return. Notice how they change in different contexts. This isn't easy at first, but it becomes more natural with practice. I know, sometimes it feels like walking, chewing gum, patting your head, and rubbing your stomach all at the same time. The more you observe different groups and cultures, the easier it becomes to notice behavior that is unique to an individual, context, group, or culture—all of which influence how a person behaves. The true artistry of observing lies in knowing what to watch.

- Watch for repeating behaviors (patterns) that tell you a person's baseline behavior. Note any behavior that is different from the baseline.

- Watch how a person interacts with others. Based on their behaviors, what reactions did he or she receive?

- Watch how all parties involved are breathing. A sudden change in breathing is a cross-cultural reaction when a baseline behavior or cultural norm has been violated. This is a classic nonverbal cue of being shocked or startled by what was just seen or heard. You can watch breathing without looking too strange by looking for the signs of a breathing change, such as the head moving forward and back with the exhale and inhale, the shoulders moving in time, and/or the chest expanding. Something outside the baseline has happened when you see someone's head tip back quickly and shoulders rise suddenly. You may not know if it was the individual's baseline, the group's baseline, or the cultural norm that was breached, but it should be noted.

The *Owner's Manual* gives telltale signs of how someone wishes to be treated. Understanding how someone views and moves through life gives you a better opportunity to make a real connection and build a lasting relationship. One way to understand others better is to observe their behaviors as they interact within a group. Before beginning your observations, ask yourself these questions:

- Do they all know each other?
- If so, how well do they know each other—just met, acquaintance, coworker, or friend?
- What are some of the behaviors displayed? How large or small are the gestures that are the norm for this group? What is the dominant voice pattern, tone, volume, and so forth? How much eye contact is normal for the group?
- Do they value members' well-being within the group or do they value getting things done?

- Take time to understand the interactions of an individual with the group as a whole and with its individual members. Notice if there are shared gestures and movements. What is the level of rapport with members of the group?

Also, look for ways to verify what you are seeing. It can be difficult to discern the correct information with minimal observation. The longer you watch, the more patterns you'll begin to see emerge. Is the pattern unique to one person or one context? Is it part of a larger behavior pattern, known as baseline behavior or group culture?

EXERCISE: OBSERVE NONVERBAL COMMUNICATION

People communicate on many levels. Begin to align your nonverbal communication with your words by learning to recognize how people communicate. Notice what does and doesn't work. Watch the people around you, particularly the ones you see as effective communicators. Use this list to direct your attention when you notice a nonverbal. Record how it was used and how it made you feel.

Nonverbal Communication	What You Noticed	How It Made You Feel
Intentional gestures		
Eye contact		
Voice pattern		
Expressions		
Body movement		
Posture, including where they place their hands and distribute their weight		
Other nonverbals, for example, how close or far away they are when they communicate		
Notice the intentional gestures to which you were drawn, and begin to incorporate those into your conversations. Notice how it makes you feel. Watch for positive nonverbal cues in response.		

The key to being good at observing is to simply notice without adding a value judgment, such as "Sally looks mad." The label *mad* comes from observing Sally's arms crossed over her chest and a furrowed brow. Our brain uses these labels as shorthand based on our experiences, which are not necessarily related to Sally. Assigning an emotional label to behaviors or a situation can cause you to misjudge.

The brain's sorting system likes to work from **labels.** As we observe something, the brain wants to say, *Oh, that is like this memory . . . file it over there with similar memories.* If we are too quick to label a behavior, we can cloud our observations. It is always best to avoid labeling what you are observing, other than the specific behavior label—such as open palm gesture, rapid breathing, or credible voice pattern. Avoid words like mad, happy, sad, angry, joyful, and other labels that assign a positive or negative value. Labeling based on emotion is part of your snap (value) judgment system, and will bias your view going forward. The snap judgment happens before you have a word or label for what you just saw. Reflect on your snap judgment and ask yourself, *Is it true? Is it real?* We all come with emotions tied to certain behaviors. Oftentimes snap judgments are not correct for several reasons:

- There's incongruence between what was seen and heard.
- You are unfamiliar with the context or baseline behaviors.
- You're unaware of the emotions at the time.
- You've developed a faulty perception or understanding.
- You have a belief system that does not allow for that particular behavior.

Even though most of us know that snap judgments can be highly flawed, we often have a gut feeling about something. The brain deletes, distorts, and generalizes to create snap judgments. This is why I warn you throughout the book to observe patterns of behavior within context and do not consider just a single behavior, movement, or gesture. Reading others has its challenges. It takes diligence to stay in the role of interested bystander without making snap or value judgments.

Final Thoughts: Master Your Message—Next Steps

Each time you make a commitment to learn something new, you grow and change. We've covered a lot of new ideas and concepts here, and while it might seem challenging to incorporate it all into your daily life, the rewards will be well worth the time and effort you devote to learning these processes. You now hold powerful knowledge: rare is the leader who is the master of his message. Intentional gestures and nonverbal communication are an integral part of leadership that is often overlooked.

In this book I have presented the more universal intentional gestures. These, like any skill, are mastered over time, through practice and trial and error. The more you exercise and evaluate what works for you—and the more you adapt what was at first less than successful—the more you'll train your unconscious to automatically use intentional gestures. Construct your own set of intentional gestures and use them, then later deconstruct what you saw, heard, and felt as you used them. Ideally, the message you send will correspond with the response you get.

It's always disappointing when you get a reaction that differs from the one you were seeking. Nevertheless, no matter what you do or say, nothing works every time—due to the integrated nature of communication. You are only one part of the equation, so remember to remain flexible and adapt your choices of intentional gestures. As you develop your own nonverbal repertoire, you will see how intentional gestures increase your influence, enhance your ability to persuade, and support your message.

It's been an honor to write a book that will serve as a solid foundation and reference guide as you become the master of your message. The question now is what are you going to do with what you have learned? Throughout the book and at the end are exercises designed to help you master what your body is saying. Cheat Sheets at the end of the book give you immediate steps to nonverbal mastery. You will also find a list of resources, including some from John Wiley & Sons, this book's publisher and one of the larger and better publishers of business and communication materials today. Take time to discover what is available to further your success.

To that end, I have set up a learning environment full of video demonstrations of the examples presented in this book, as well as a more detailed list of resources, articles, and exercises so that you can continue to get support and advice about the concepts I've laid out in this book, at www.WhatYourBodySays.com. After all, this book is only the beginning. No book can do justice to the training ground that is the real world. I encourage you to visit often as I update the website with the processes and concepts I observe every day. While this may be the end of the book, it certainly isn't the end of this chapter. You will be changing and growing, gaining new insights every day. Practice and attention are the keys to mastery. As a personal mentor, I can offer support that will inspire you to take action and master your nonverbal message.

I hope these principles, techniques, and strategies for using intentional gestures to become a masterful communicator make a true difference in your life and the lives of those you touch. I look forward to hearing about your success. Take time to drop me a note about what you have accomplished after reading this book. Let me post your story on my website so that others may learn from your success. Learning is a generative and ongoing process, and the world belongs to the person willing to continually learn. I sincerely thank you for spending time with me as you learn *What Your Body Says (and how to master the message)*. You now have the tools to be a masterful communicator—so go share who you are with the world and have a wonder-filled time whatever your next adventure may be!

Sharon Sayler

P.S. More information and resources are available at www.WhatYourBodySays.com.

Cheat Sheets

1. **How to Project Confidence**
   - Move with intent. Weight evenly centered over hips whether moving or not.
   - Use more eye contact than you normally do. Limit blinking.
   - Be slow to smile.
   - Use side palm hand gestures to punctuate what you are saying.
   - When not speaking, hold arms either at your sides or parallel to the ground.
   - Use the connection voice for relationships and the credible voice for business.
   - Use clear articulation and pacing of the words—a calm cadence.
   - Use short pauses between segments of statements and a longer pause at end of each statement.
   - Maintain low natural breathing.

2. How to Look Intelligent

- Maintain low natural breathing. Breathe only through your nose, no mouth breathing.

- Pause longer and more frequently than you normally would.

- Use more eye contact than you normally do. Limit blinking.

- Be slow to smile.

- When speaking, maintain a steady, still hand gesture that fits what you are saying.

- Hold a gesture in place throughout a pause, except for negative news.

- Keep your gesture, head, and lips still during the pause.

- When you are not speaking, keep arms either at your sides or parallel to the ground.

- Use the connection voice for relationships and the credible voice for business.

- Use clear articulation and pacing of the words—a calm cadence.

- Use a short pause between segments of statements and a longer pause at end of each statement.

- When seated, keep your forearms comfortably on the table, hands resting together but not clasped.

3. How to Deliver Your Message

- Choreograph your gestures to your message before important speaking engagements.

- Know the outcome you want from your conversation. Think before you talk.

- Know your audience and, if possible, their viewpoint and level of understanding about the subject matter.

- Get to the point quickly and use gestures that relate to your point.

- Hold a gesture in place throughout a pause, except for negative news.

- Maintain low natural breathing.

- Pause longer and more frequently than you normally would.

- Keep your gesture, head, and lips still during the pause.

- When you are not speaking, keep arms either at your sides or parallel to the ground.

- Use the connection voice for relationships and the credible voice for business.

- Use clear articulation and pacing of the words—a calm cadence.

- Use a short silent pause between segments of statements and a longer pause at the end of each statement.

4. **How to Eliminate the Verbal Pause**

   Audible pauses, such as *ah, um,* and *you know,* muddle your message and reduce your credibility.

   - Keep breathing. Maintain low natural breathing.

   - Fill the silence with a gesture and/or smile.

   - Use shorter sentences.

   - Eliminate the reasons for audible pauses, which include lack of familiarity with the topic, discomfort with silence, nervousness, or habit.

   - Practice beforehand. Record yourself and listen for your favorite verbal pause fillers.

5. **How to Create the Credible Voice Pattern**

- Use clear articulation and pacing of words.

- Maintain a calm cadence.

- Maintain a flat sound until the end of the phrase or sentence. Drop the chin slightly as you end each sentence.

- Use short pauses between sections of each sentence (where the comma would go) and longer pauses at the end of each statement (where the period would go).

- During each pause, breathe. Inhale completely filling the abdomen, keeping your head and lips perfectly still.

- To emphasize the key point maintain direct eye contact longer than normal. Limit blinking but do not stare.

- If the message is open to discussion and you want to stress importance, use a sideways palm hand gesture. If not open to negotiation, use a palm down gesture.

- If standing, have your weight on both feet. Posture is erect.

- If sitting, have your weight centered over your sit bones, and sit on the first one-third to two-thirds of the chair.

6. **How to Create the Connection Voice Pattern**

- Use clear articulation and pacing of words. Maintain a calm, rhythmic pattern that flows up and down.

- End each statement with the voice going up—similar to a question mark. Move your chin up about one inch as you complete your sentence.

- Lightly bob your head as your voice flows up and down in a rhythmic pattern.

- Use short pauses between sections of each statement and a longer pause at the end of each statement.

- During the pause, breathe. The body and head can move.
- Use gestures of relationship.
- Make a connection with natural, casual eye contact. Looking away from time to time is normal.
- Mirror and match the listener's behaviors to establish rapport.
- Avoid paraphrasing, as different words often have different meanings.
- If standing, your weight does not need to be evenly on both feet. If sitting, your back can touch the back of the chair or you can sit slightly off center.

7. **How to Handle the Heckler**
   - Maintain low natural breathing.
   - First, try ignoring—sometimes no attention will extinguish behavior.
   - If behavior continues, verbally remind. For example, "Please hold questions until our Q&A time." Use palm down gesture.
   - Use the credible voice pattern—flat tone drops at the end of phrase.
   - If behavior continues, look to opposite side of the audience (away from) and nonverbally gesture to wait in hecklers direction. The wait gesture is:
     - Move your arm closest to the heckler straight down your side.
     - Slowly bend your arm at the elbow to move your forearm about 30 degrees up from your side.
     - With your palm facing down, slightly cock your wrist back to expose your fingertips.

- Hold that gesture as you continue presentation. Do not drop the gesture until the behavior has stopped for a while.

- Withhold eye contact from heckler. Keep your gaze on the rest of the audience.

- Weight evenly centered over hips whether moving or not.

- When not speaking, hold arms either at your sides or parallel to the ground.

8. **How to Use Your Posture to Show Your Confidence in Others**

- Back straight to create erect posture.

- Shoulders square on spine and back, no slouching shoulders.

- Head squarely above shoulders and neck.

- Chin parallel to ground.

- Eyes open and focused on where you are going.

- Weight even on both legs if standing.

- Gait steady and smooth if walking.

- Breathing low and steady, with smooth abdominal movement.

- Three positions of your forearms: waist-high in front of your body, both arms at your side, or the combination (one arm at your side and the other forearm at your waist parallel to the ground).

9. **How to Motivate Others**

- Maintain low natural breathing.

- Understand and use their preferred sensory modalities of visual, auditory, kinesthetic/tactile.

- Use more eye contact than you normally do.

- Smile.

- Use a palm up gesture to seek information or make a request.

- Use sideways palm gesture for key points.

- Use palm down to assign tasks.

- When not gesturing, keep arms either at your sides or parallel to the ground.

- Use the connection voice for relationships, the credible voice for business.

- Use a short pause between segments of statements and a longer pause at end of each statement.

- Use sincere praise for a job well done.

10. **How to Diffuse a Situation**

- Maintain low, steady breathing.

- Listen. Look down and nod your head to indicate listening.

- Decrease eye contact during emotions and increase eye contact during recovery stage. Direct eye contact can enflame the situation.

- Use a visual placeholder as a neutral. Having a visual to look at during the time allows for eye contact to be directed other than face-to-face.

- Use the other person's words. Do not paraphrase.

- Speak in third-person about event. Use pronouns he/she or the situation.

- Speak in first-person about the relationship.

- Hold arms at your sides or parallel to the ground.

- Speak only when the outburst is over, indicated by a change in the other person's breathing.

- Understand and use their preferred sensory modalities of visual, auditory, kinesthetic/tactile.

- Use side palm hand gestures to indicate this is serious.

- Use open palm up hand gestures to seek more information.

- Position body at 90 degrees from the other person—not face-to-face or across desk/table.

- Use credible voice pattern to speak of the event and maintain control.

- Use connection voice pattern to speak when looking at the person and when emotional control is regained.

- Use clear articulation and pacing of the words—a calm cadence.

- Use a short pause between segments of statements and a longer pause at end of each statement.

11. How to Nonverbally Request Someone Slow Down or Wait

- Make sure your weight is on both feet.

- Breathe low and from the abdomen to get oxygen to the brain.

- Turn your shoulders and/or feet away from the speaker.

- To create the wait hand gesture:

  1. Slowly bend at the elbow—about 30 degrees up from your side.

  2. With your palm facing down, slightly cock your wrist back just to expose your fingertips.

  3. Hold the gesture frozen in that position until your mind has a chance to catch up and your thoughts are clear.

12. **How to Deliver Bad News and Survive**

- Maintain low steady breathing.

- Have a visual placeholder for bad news.

- Limit eye contact for bad news. Use eye contact for relationship building.

- Use credible voice pattern to speak of the bad news and maintain control.

- Use connection voice pattern to speak about the relationship.

- Clear articulation and pacing of the words—a calm cadence.

- Short pause between segments of statement and a longer pause at end of each statement.

- Use the person's words. Do not paraphrase.

- Speak only when they recover from hearing bad news indicated by a change in their breathing.

- Speak in third-person about bad news, such as *the* bad news and not *your* bad news.

- Keep arms at your sides or parallel to the ground when standing.

- No elbows on the table if seated.

- Use side palm hand gestures to indicate this is serious.

- Use palm down gestures to indicate not open to negotiation.

- Use open palm up to seek more information and build the personal relationship.

- Position body at 90 degrees. Not face-to-face or across from each other as if seated at a desk.

Resources and Recommended Reading

For a complete list of communication, business relationship, and leadership resources mentioned in this book, along with hundreds of others, please log onto www.WhatYourBodySays.com and go to the Resources section.

Eisenberg, Bryan, and Jeffrey, *Waiting for Your Cat to Bark?* Nashville: Thomas Nelson, Inc., 2006.

Goleman, Daniel. *Emotional Intelligence.* New York: Bantam Books, 2006.

Goleman, Daniel. *Social Intelligence.* New York: Bantam Books, 2006.

Grinder, Michael. *Charisma: The Art of Relationships.* Battle Ground, WA: Michael Grinder and Associates, 2004.

Grinder, Michael. *The Elusive Obvious.* Battle Ground, WA: Michael Grinder and Associates, 2007.

Grinder, Michael. *Managing Groups*. Battle Ground, WA: Michael Grinder and Associates, 2008.

Lakhani, Dave. *Persuasion*. Hoboken, NJ: John Wiley & Sons, 2005.

Mehrabian, Albert. *Nonverbal Communication*. Chicago: Aldine-Atherton, 1972.

Mehrabian, Albert. *Silent Messages: Implicit Communication of Emotions and Attitudes* (2nd ed). Belmont, CA: Wadsworth, 1981.

NeuroLinguistic programming (NLP)—any original work by Richard Bandler and John Grinder, or the multitude of sources that have sprung from their work. Consider:

Dilts, Robert, and DeLozier, Judith. *Encyclopedia of Systemic NLP and NLP New Coding*. Scotts Valley, CA: NLP University Press, 2000.

Grinder, John, and Bandler, Richard. *The Structure of Magic: A Book About Language and Therapy*. Palo Alto, CA: Science and Behavior Books, 1989.

Molden, David. *Managing the Power of NLP*. Upper Saddle River, NJ: Pearson Education Limited, 2007.

Phillips, Gary. *The Art of Safety*. Thunder Bay, Ontario, Canada: OH&S Press, 2006.

Port, Michael. *Book Yourself Solid*. Hoboken, NJ: John Wiley & Sons, 2006.

Port, Michael. *Think Big Manifesto*. Hoboken, NJ: John Wiley & Sons, 2009.

Riveness, David T. *The Secret Life of the Corporate Jester*. Santa Clara, CA: Jardin Publishing, 2006.

Quick Reference
Guides

Practicing Nonverbal Communication
Like anything else you desire to learn, you will have to practice consciously adding nonverbal elements to your daily communication. Take it one day at a time. Practice one skill a week—study it, practice it, and begin to own it.

Nonverbal	Exercise	Practice
Chapter 3, Gestures of Relationship	With a friend use the palm up, sideways palm, and the down palm gesture, with one arm and then both arms. Now, reverse and have your friend do the gestures toward you while you observe.	How does it make you feel to do each gesture? How does it feel to receive each gesture? How did your friend feel receiving each gesture?

Chapter 4, Gestures of Location	With a friend practice gesturing to a location while giving bad news using the palm up, sideways palm, and the palm down, with one arm and then both arms. Now, reverse and have your friend do the gestures toward you while you observe.	How does it feel to do each gesture? How does it feel to view each gesture? How did your friend feel receiving each gesture?
Chapter 5, Gestures That Teach	Think of several gestures that you would use to teach someone about something you know how to do. Remember to start on your right, as if the viewer across from you sees the mirror image.	Practice with a friend or view in a mirror. Were you able to keep it systematic and consistent? Ask your friend for feedback.
Chapter 6, Gestures of Expectation and Influence	Use the three arm positions for self-confidence and the five gestures not to do.	Note which of the three arm positions feels most natural to you. Practice what to do and what not to do. Notice how each position makes you feel.
Some of these may come more easily than others. Practice one new skill a week, and then practice putting them together to make new nonverbal patterns to support your message.		

Chapter 7: The Eyes Have It

Eye contact can be subtle or direct. Knowing how to mix the two is a major part of the art of influencing and empowering others.

Where Do I Put My Eyes?	Exercise	Practice
Business eye contact, direct your eyes between the listener's eyes or just a bit higher. Imagine a triangle with the base below the listener's eyes and the peak of the triangle at their mid-forehead.	Ask a friend to help you. Stand facing each other and look in each other's eyes. Simply be with that person. Notice what goes on with you and how comfortable or uncomfortable you feel.	Learn the difference between professional and personal eye placement. Practice each in the appropriate situation. Notice how it feels to you and notice the difference it makes in your exchange.
Relationship or personal eye contact has more latitude. Invert the triangle so the peak is now at the other person's mouth.	Notice your own eye contact in social and business situations. See if you can increase your ability to gently maintain eye contact. Now, look away. Notice what the other person does.	Did you notice any changes in your breathing or your friend's with prolonged direct eye contact? What is going on with you when you feel the need to break eye contact? Just notice what motivates you to look away.
Manage with Eye Contact	**Exercise**	**Practice**
Direct eye contact with the dropped chin, eyes high in the eye sockets says "Stop"—you are being judged or watched.	Notice how the eye contact and facial expressions make you feel.	Practice with a friend, dropping your chin and direct eye contact. Try various facial expressions.

Eye Contact and Emotions	Exercise	Practice
If the topic is emotional or intense, break eye contact on occasion to allow both of you to breathe. (Of course, if the emotional stability of the listener or your safety is an issue, eye contact is necessary.) Use visual placeholders or locations to place bad news.	While speaking with a friend, ask him/her to watch your eye contact. Notice how it feels when you look at the listener's eyes and when looking at a visual placeholder.	Practice giving yourself some bad news in the mirror. Practice using locations to see how you can add a gesture of location to move the bad news away from being associated with you.

Chapter 8: How the Signals Sound—The Voice

The nonverbals behind the voice, including breathing, are the best opportunity for building influence, trust, and safety in a business relationship. Most people have a similar understanding of what tones, volumes, and other nonverbals of the speaking voice should be. The common nonverbal components of voice include:

- Tone: warm, cool, bored, upbeat.
- Pitch: flat, low, high, ending up or down.
- Emphasis: too much, too little, where it is placed.
- Volume: too loud, too soft, just right, forced.
- Speed: pacing, tempo, cadence, rhythm.
- Culture: accent, pronunciations, slang, clichés.
- Emotion: happy, sad, afraid, excited, nervous.
- Facial expressions: smile, clenched jaw.
- Clarity: mumbling, stuttering, enunciation.
- Pause: verbal, silent, length.
- Breathing: shallow, rapid, comfortable, forced, hesitant.

Of course, this is just a partial list of all the ways you can change your voice.

Monotone voice	Considered dull to listen to, vary your voice.	Pretend you have a paintbrush in your hand and are painting a tall fence. Start talking as you paint. When you paint up high, use a higher pitch and when you paint down low, use a lower pitch. Play with this to expand your range. When you speak, you are painting a picture with your words.
Forced or announcer	Sounds strange and artificial.	This tonality occurs when you have distanced yourself from the person with whom you are speaking. To get rid of this tone, you have to make an internal change by allowing yourself to become more connected. To hear the difference, pretend you are talking to a friend and see what happens.
Too loud or too soft	No one likes to be yelled at or struggle to hear.	This is a matter of self-awareness. Notice how your voice quality changes when you speak too loud or too softly.
Too fast or too slow	Fast talkers are fast listeners. That does not mean that slow talkers are slow learners, but it does affect how you must communicate with them.	Observe yourself. Watch for the baseline or normal speed of various cultures. If possible, try to match speed without looking fake. It doesn't have to be exact.

Have nonverbals match your words	You can make your point by changing the emphasis on a word or words.	Use pitch, volume, and cadence to emphasize words and phrases. If you are working from a script, mark in bold or underline words you want to emphasize. If you are working from an outline, mark in bold or underline words that have the most meaning. If you are in a conversation, be certain that the listener understands what you are saying by your choice of words and emphasis from the sound and length of pause.
Pause	Pauses can be verbal or silent and can vary in length depending on the message.	There is an art to the pause. Practice the silent, gestured pause.
Breathing	Can be high, low, comfortable, forced, hesitant, or rapid.	This is the foundation of all your communication. Review and practice low, abdominal breathing.

Chapter 8: Voice Patterns of What We Do and Who We Are		
Voice Pattern	**What Your Voice Does**	**What Your Body Does**
Credible Accentuates your status, sends information, and emphasizes parts of your message.	Use clear articulation and pacing of the words. Maintain a calm cadence. Maintain a flat tone. During the pause, breathe. Drop the chin slightly as you end each phrase or statement.	As you come to the part of the message you want to emphasize, maintain direct eye contact longer than normal and limit blinking, but do not stare. If the message is serious, use a palm sideways hand gesture. If it is not open to discussion, use a palm down hand gesture. If standing, have your weight on both feet. Posture is erect. Keep your forearms at your sides or waist high in front of your body, resting at your natural waist, or one forearm at your side and the other bent and resting at your natural waist.
Connection Used to seek information, soften the news, and create the emotional connection. Builds relationships.	Use clear articulation and pacing of the words. Maintain a calm and rhythmic pattern. Bob your head with the voice as it rolls up and down with the rhythmic pattern. Use shorter pauses than the credible voice. Voice goes up at the end similar to asking a question. During the pause, breathe. Inhale completely.	Most common gestures are the palm open, facing up. If the message is serious and speaking about the relationship, use a sideways palm gesture. Keep your forearms at your sides or waist high in front of your body, resting at your natural waist, or one forearm at your side and the other bent, resting at your natural waist. Make normal eye contact. It is okay to look away on occasion. Mirror and match the listener's movements. Weight can be uneven over the hips.

Chapter 8: Breathing Patterns and How Others Perceive Us

There are two main types of breathing patterns. Each one affects how others experience us.

Breathing Pattern	How Others Experience Us	Practice
Shallow, high, or rapid breathing is most often perceived by others as distress, anger, fear, startle, or surprise.	Verbally, those stuck in the shallow, high, or rapid breathing pattern are at a loss for words and use fill-in sounds, such as *uhm* and *ahh,* as they try to continue to talk.	Notice your breathing under stress, particularly if you start to add the verbal pause. Place your hand in the area of your navel to monitor for low breathing. That will center you and bring your breathing back to normal.
The low and abdominal breathing pattern is the natural pattern in normal situations. Strive to maintain even during periods of stress.	Supports the tone and projects a calm, in-charge persona.	Practice this to recognize what it feels like. Lie on your back and place your hand over your navel and begin to breathe in a manner that moves your hand up and down.

Chapter 9: The Fidget Reboot

Nervous, fidgety, or anxious behaviors make others uneasy.

Common Fidgets	Practice the Fidget Reboot Button
■ Touching the face and neck. ■ Stroking or smoothing the hair. ■ High chest breathing, shallow breathing. ■ Clicking a pen or picking at fingernails. ■ Playing with jewelry. ■ Deep breath blowing out through the mouth. ■ Licking, rolling lips in or biting lips. ■ Picking at or cleaning lint off clothes.	Become consciously aware of, and control, how you are breathing. Work to maintain low, slow abdominal breathing. Breathing is key to most of your nonverbal success. 1. Center your weight. To center your weight, feel your strength and most of your weight in the space between your navel and groin. 2. Look straight ahead with your chin level to the ground. Have your throat as open as possible. 3. Take a slow, easy, deep breath and gently hold it. You should feel and see your abdomen (below the rib cage) expand. 4. Gently exhale through your nose until you see and feel the abdomen deflate. 5. Pause, your body will gently tell you when it is time to breathe again. 6. Repeat until you feel calmness settle over you. 7. Repeat. You will begin to notice clear thinking returns as the carbon dioxide and oxygen levels get back in balance.

How to Successfully Review Yourself on Video

Video is the quickest way to accelerate your understanding of what your body is saying. At first, it may feel uncomfortable. The longer you review video of yourself the easier it becomes to see nonverbals. To capture yourself on video and observe your nonverbals, have a conversation with a friend while you sit in front of a video camera. Choose several topics, for example, one that excites you, one that concerns or angers you, some friendly, some serious. You're looking for something that will create a shift in your emotions. Review the tape four times as follows:

What to Look For	What You Saw and How You Could Change the Message
First viewing: Comment on whatever you want. Don't just think it, write out what you see, feel, and think.	
Second viewing: Observe in the third-person. Use statements such as "she/he did" when referring to yourself.	
Third viewing: With the observations from the second viewing, comment on what you would do differently if you were the person (third-person) you are watching.	
Fourth viewing: Listen for content. Write down all the points that are unclear or need support.	

Index